W9-CES-974

ENEMY IN THE PEW?

ENEMY

IN THE PEW?

Daniel D. Walker

HARPER & ROW, PUBLISHERS

New York, Evanston, and London

Biblical quotations are from the Revised Standard Version of the Bible, copyright 1946 and 1952 by the Division of Christian Education of the National Council of the Churches of Christ in the U.S.A., and from J. P. Phillips' *The Gospels* (1957), *Letters to Young Churches* (1952), and *The Young Church in Action* (1955), published by The Macmillan Company. Unless otherwise indicated, the quotations are from the Revised Standard Version.

LIBRARY OF CONGRESS CATALOG CARD NUMBER: 67-14938

TO FIVE YOUNG LAYMEN

RAISED IN PARSONAGES:

Jerry and June

Doug

Lois Ann

Tom

Contents

Preface

The ministry is a vocation. So is the laity. Both confirmation and ordination involve a commitment to full-time Christian living.

This book has been written to help the layman know his job and feel its challenge. Its purpose is to direct him beyond the tensions and frustrations of church work to the enduring satisfactions of discipleship through the church.

There is a sense in which *Enemy in the Pew?* is a companion volume to *The Human Problems of the Minister*, published by Harper & Row in 1960. In the preface to that book I stated, "The basic question that runs throughout the book is, 'What is the role of the minister in our generation?' " In *Enemy in the Pew?* we shift from pulpit to pew and ask essentially the same question: "What is the role of the *layman* in our generation?" The role is changing rapidly, and there is a need to understand what the changes are and what they mean.

Some writers take a hopeless view of what is ahead for the church. I do not. There are problems, but they can be faced and handled. God is not dead. The church is not a pawn in *The Secular City*. Thousands of churchmen do not find the pew very "comfortable." Many laymen have already thawed out if indeed they ever were *God's Frozen People*. And the ranks of Christian churchmen have been full of people who were *Honest to God* long before Bishop Robinson ever thought of writing a book by that title and will continue to be so in spite of such books.

The Human Problems of the Minister was about the ministry, but it was for the edification of both ministers and laymen. *Enemy in the Pew?* is about the laity, who need not only to understand themselves but to be understood by their ministers. So this book, too, is addressed to both the ordained and the unordained.

It is not theological in the academic sense of the word. However, I have tried to nourish its roots in reality in the hope that its fruits are good. You may describe the book however you like. I think of it as a book for people hoping, through the church, to realize God's will in their lives and in the world.

Most books carry the name of a single author, but none is the result of one man's work. This book is no exception. My parents started it when they brought me into a church-related home. My wife and children contributed much, as did those fine men and women who have shared staff responsibilities with me in each of my local church assignments. But mostly I am indebted to the many laymen, great and undeveloped, loyal and indifferent, in whose fellowship I have been privileged to serve. In ways known and unknown, recognizable and disguised, these grand people live in the pages of this book.

The staff and membership of The First Methodist Church of Santa Monica and The First Methodist Church of Pasadena, both in California, must have special mention. These are the people in whose company my ideas took shape and whose patience and encouragement saw me through the writing process. The important job of typing the manuscript was done by my able secretary, Thelma Livoti.

It is customary, when thanking those who have read one's manuscript and made "many helpful suggestions," to relieve them of all responsibility for the final contents. I'm not going to let David McKeithen off the hook that easily. He read, he helped, and he also agreed. At least that's what he told me. I am quite willing to assume full responsibility for all that I have written here, but it is reassuring that this admired friend and ministerial colleague is quick to say that his thoughts completely confirm my own.

My greatest indebtedness is to Virginia, my wife. Technically a "layman," she has, since our marriage in 1941, shared every aspect of her husband's ministry. Her editorial assistance, though great, is secondary to her constant encouragement and inspiration.

Pasadena, California

DANIEL D. WALKER

I

The Revolution in the Church

There is a revolution in the church, and all of us should be aware of it. Creeds are crumbling and ecclesiastical systems are falling apart.

Missionary concepts have changed. The idea that a missionary is a white Westerner out to convert the dark-skinned heathen in pagan lands is as out of date as grandmother's gramophone.

The theological climate keeps shifting. It requires almost as tricky a sense of timing for the minister to keep abreast of the latest theological fads as for his wife to lift or lower her hemline in response to the authoritative voice of fashion.

The church as an institution is under such severe criticism that people are asking whether it should be saved or abandoned. One Methodist Bishop says, "The church is sick at the core, and no readjustments of organization will suffice" to cure it.

Some forty years ago George Santayana predicted that "Romantic Christendom," as he called it—referring, I suppose, to the westernized institutions of Christianity, our village churches and city cathedrals, our well-dressed Easters and sentimental Christmases—"may be coming to an end." More recently, Martin E. Marty, church historian and writer, has struck that same note. He says that "place-inhabiting Christendom" (that is, the church building as a center of religious activity) is "an episode" that is passing. One parish minister states that the institutional structure of the church is so far gone that it is "not renewable" and has become a hindrance "to the proclamation of the Gospel." Believe me—there is a revolution going on in the church!

How is the layman to react to it?

Certainly not by *ignoring* it. The church is in for radical readjustment, and the process will not be stopped merely because we do not notice it. I may choose to ignore the heavy traffic passing my church on Colorado Boulevard, but that doesn't thin it out or slow it down. It just makes me a likely candidate for stretcher space in an ambulance. To ignore the revolution in the church is to volunteer as one of its casualties.

Resenting it is no better. Most of us are tempted to accept change with reluctance, as though it were as evil as it is inevitable. But dragging feet are of no help to the Christian church. Reluctant acceptance of change only adds despair to the other strains of adjustment. It is useless to resent the inevitable.

Merely to *observe* the revolution is no smarter way to react to it. There is nothing commendable about stepping to the sidelines to wait it out, expecting to board the victory train when the revolution has been won. Anyone using that tactic will be left standing with his bundle of pale memories at an abandoned railroad station. The church will not travel the old track again.

What, then, is the layman to do? He must react to the

revolution by becoming a revolutionist! If reform is in order, then he, like Luther, should be a reformer. If the organized church is too stuffy and tradition-bound to appeal to modern man, then like Wesley, the Christian layman should lead the exodus and head for the streets and open fields. If the temple needs cleansing, the churchman's place is beside the Christ who upset tables of tradition and drove out those who made the church indistinguishable from the society around it. His place is with the revolutionists.

In that position, his first responsibility is to learn the aims of the revolution. Unfortunately no one can define them exactly. Revolutions erupt with violence and settle in disorder. Nevertheless there is purpose in them, and for all of their messy way of doing business they reveal a clear antipathy for one thing and an affection for another. Always there is something they seek to "overcome," as the battle hymn of the Civil Rights movement reminds us. And there is something else they would put in its place. Sometimes it is easier to see what they want to destroy than what they would build. But invariably the true revolution combines the demand for freedom from that which can no longer be tolerated with hope of achieving that which must no longer be withheld. So, while no detailed blueprint is available for the revolution in the church, the general hates and hopes of it are discernible. Seeing these, the lay revolutionists will combine their efforts to move the church away from the one and toward the other.

To begin with, the revolution calls for a shift from activity to depth.

A sociologist has written a book about the modern church and entitled it, *The Noise of Solemn Assemblies*. Our churches *are* noisy. With endless fellowship, dialogue, programs, projects, and special activities, we have moved away from the life Jesus was talking about when he told Martha she was too busy and that Mary had chosen "the better part." The meditative prayer experience of the Christian mystic has become an eccentricity among us. The need for greater spiritual depth is still there, but when we feel it, we do not seek the solitude that gives it birth. We organize a group to talk about it! Incredible as it may seem, it is an uphill struggle to quiet the conversation in many church sanctuaries. Designed for meditation and prayer, these rooms often rumble with our compulsion to converse.

"One of the principles of the Hindu religion is to refrain from useless conversation," my ninth-grade daughter said to me one day when I was chattering on about something unimportant. I was properly rebuked. We should never waste words. Especially in church, trivial chatter should be eliminated. But unfortunately, for many of us, silence is a vacuum to be filled with sound, and time is a static state to be filled with vigorous activity. We keep our tongues flapping and our feet in perpetual motion and call this jumble of misdirected energy our religious life.

This results in contradiction. We preach composure and practice confusion. We talk about the values of a meditative life and keep too busy to meditate. We consult our date books more than our Bibles and substitute activity for depth. We are overorganized, overinstitutionalized, overfellowshiped, and under too much pressure. We send too many Christmas cards, make too many phone calls, subscribe to too many magazines, and attend too many meetings. We are so addicted to chatter that even when observing the ritual of grace at table, we sometimes plunge into conversation again before the final consonant is sounded on the amen.

The great men of the Bible found their security in God. We feel safer in a crowd. Leaving the crowd behind, Moses scaled the mountain to meet his Maker. John went to the desert alone to fast and to listen for the voice of God from deep in the awesome silence. Isaiah entered the temple to be alone with God. A wonderful passage in the Gospel of John that tells how the crowds gathered around Jesus to hear his prophetic teaching, concludes with these words:

"When Jesus had said this, he departed and *hid himself* from them" (John 12:36b). Comes the revolution, and we shall learn to hide even from our church friends.

This does not mean we are heartless. We all know how painful loneliness can be, and are well aware of the church's responsibility to offer friendship to the friendless. We know that man is a social being who must experience meaningful relationships or lose his sanity. It does not follow from this, however, that everyone who enters the church must be tackled by a friendly greeter, or be sucked into participation in a "face-to-face" group, or become "involved" in the work of a commission. What some people need most is the right to remain anonymous. The increasing number of homes that are built with a windowless wall to the street, and the growing numbers of persons requesting unlisted telephone numbers are signs of the times we ought not to miss. Along with the growing army of apartment house dwellers who not only do not know the others who live at the same address, but have no desire to know them, these people are acting out in daily life their deep need for solitude. They are neither hostile nor aloof. They are normal human beings, trying to experience more of life's quality by imposing some limits on its quantity.

That indicates the direction the revolution must take. We already know how to mingle with people; now we must learn how to hide from them. We believe in the open-door policy; we want everyone to feel welcome and know that ours is "The Friendly Church." But we must learn how to lock the door and silence the phone.

The reason we must do this is not just to quiet our nerves and gain peace of mind. We must do it for the Gospel's sake. Our confused world needs men of deep understanding who can penetrate sham and distinguish truth from half-truth. But such men are not born in confusion. They emerge from the soul's quietness. That is why the Spanish philosopher, Ortega y Gasset, declaring that truth is a casualty of our busy world, said, "Without a certain margin of tranquility, truth succumbs." Quietness and truth belong together. How simply the Psalmist puts it, "Be still and know . . .!" (Ps. 46:10). In quietness, life's sediment settles; the petty things that muddied the waters sink from sight, and true values become apparent. On the frontier of tranquility the mists of vagueness and confusion lift, and life's purpose emerges unblurred. That's why we must shift from talking to listening. We must set sail on the seas of silence. We must discover our "margin of tranquility." Once more the church should become the Christian's haven of peace. It should be natural for him to slip into the church courtyard on a warm afternoon, just to sit in a pleasant place and meditate. He should step into the chapel for the solitude of it. He should enter the sanctuary alone and let the windows tell their incomparable stories and the fingered arches offer silent prayer. The revolution must move the church from activity to depth.

A second thing the revolution in the church involves is a shift from membership to discipleship.

There is a natural tendency for us to equate membership in the church with discipleship to Jesus Christ. But they are not synonymous, and the one does not necessarily follow from the other. Membership nails us down; discipleship pulls us loose. Membership draws us in; discipleship sends us out. Membership pays its dues and claims its rights; discipleship makes any sacrifice, asking nothing in return.

Today church membership has a lot to offer. It provides a "chaplain" to call on us when we are sick and counseling to lift us over the rough places. It provides study opportunities, congenial social groups tailored to suit our age and interests, nursery care, luncheons and dinners at a modest cost, a good library, a gymnasium for sports activities, and a sense of righteousness in the illusion that in accepting these things we are somehow contributing to the poor, educating the illiterate, and building a world of peace. Membership in no other organization offers so much for so little. This is what gives the sting to the jibe that the church is the poor man's country club.

It is also what makes us realize that there is more to being Christian than keeping one's name on the church roll, one's pledge paid in full, and a generous portion of one's time given to participation in church activities. Discipleship is needed. This is more than membership.

A disciple is a Christian under orders. Reviewing the Gospels recently, I was astounded at the number of times Jesus sent his followers out to do something. The record is punctuated with terse orders: Go preach—Go sell—Go work—Go into the highways—Go into the next towns—Go into the country—Go to the other side—Go to your house—Go out into the deep—Go into the streets—Go into the city—Go into the village—Go to my brethren—Go to the lost sheep—Go call your husband—Go make it right with your brother—Go and see—Go and learn—Go quickly—Go in peace—Arise, and go!

It is natural that Jesus should put this emphasis on action, for it was built into his religious heritage. The Hebrew idea of God was born among a nomadic people, and their deepest religious insights emerged from their wanderings. Yahweh proved to be superior to rival deities at least in part because he was "mobile" while they were not. Not only did he travel with the Children of Israel; he "went before them" (Exod. 13:21). He was a God on the go.

As though designed to fit such a tradition, Jesus himself, as Harvey Cox reminds us in *The Secular City*, was "born during a journey, spent his first years in exile, was expelled from his own home town, and declared that he had no place to lay his head." It was said of his followers, who made up the first Christian church, that they had "no lasting city." They were first known as "The People of the Way."

You can see by this that Christianity was fashioned for a day like ours, for it is geared to be mobile. As twentieth-century nomads, we move from one city to another in search of improved circumstances, and we move our residence within the city for greater convenience and congeniality.

We are constantly commuting, not to our work only, but also to our recreation, to where we shop, to study courses and lectures, and to where we socialize. Indeed, the church is one of the few institutions in modern urban society which is reluctant to admit that its constituents have wheels. It assumes that people's lives center in neighborhoods and that their churches must be located within walking distance of their homes.

But modern society doesn't rotate around the village well as in Bible times, nor around the general store where our grandfathers congregated. Its nerve centers are busy airports, sprawling freeways, high-speed elevators, cars, boats, escalators, moving sidewalks, and catapulting space capsules. Modern man is on the go.

That's a good thing in itself. But it's bad for the church that sees itself as a sedentary institution, dependent upon people who stay home. That's why the shift from membership to discipleship is so crucial. A disciple is out on the road.

Does this sound contradictory to my earlier appeal for solitude? There is no contradiction, only alternation. Activity is significant as it emerges from stillness, and quietness has content in response to activity. If it is important to be alone, it is also important to mingle with the people. It is in the midst of life's commotion that the listening ear, sensitized through silence, can hear humanity's unspoken language. We should move among the people of our cities, listening not only to what they say, but also to the intonation of their voices, the silent speech of their posture, and the eloquent message of their facial expression. Our ears should be tuned to the sounds of loneliness, guilt, hunger, fear, resentment, anger, love, hope, and all those messages that come to those who hear the words no man has spoken. We should listen to the apprehensive sound of aging, the raucous blare of greed, the harmonies of faith, and the haunting cry of unborn children. And we should meet the people where they are, at business conferences, social gatherings, and political rallies; in airplanes, hotel lobbies, and in private clubs; at union meetings or picket lines, in science laboratories, and in smoke-filled rooms. The church is more than a place to "gather together to ask the Lord's blessing." It is men with a mission. The real thrust of the gospel comes not just when we "gather," but when we "go!"

And when he goes, the disciple travels "light." "Take nothing for your journey," said Jesus to his disciples, "no staff, nor bag, nor bread, nor money; and do not have two tunics" (Luke 9:3). He counseled the rich ruler to let go of the holdings that were holding him, and get on with the job of being a disciple.

That counsel may be as pertinent for the church as for the individual. Perhaps it should unload. It may need to reduce its membership to what someone has called the "hard core, cross-carrying Christians." If its real estate anchors it to a street corner and keeps it from blossoming in the homes and offices of the city, then let it dispose of all lands and buildings that are not clearly a help in spreading God's truth. If the church as an institution is too cumbersome and gets in the way of its own gospel, then let it simplify its organization. A disciple travels "light."

He also gets results. "By this my Father is glorified," said Jesus, "that you bear much fruit, and so prove to be my disciples" (John 15:8).

There are some seventy-four million of us who are members of Protestant churches in America today. How much fruit do we bear? Do we challenge our clubs and business groups to a higher type of living? Are we teaching our neighbors and business associates the meaning of interracial brotherhood? Are we finding constructive ways to guarantee every citizen access to a high quality of medical care? Are we challenging bigotry wherever we hear it expressed—in barber shop or restaurant, at the country club or across the dinner table? Are we creating among our friends and associates a climate of goodwill toward people of all nations so that our statesmen can negotiate from a position of national moral strength as they work with others to build a world of peace? If not, what makes us think we are disciples? It wasn't "belonging to the church" but "bearing much fruit" that Jesus established as proof of discipleship. If we are disciples, we get results.

We also suffer. A disciple is one who has sacrificed something. Jesus said that anyone who is not willing to go contrary to "his own father and mother and wife and children and brothers and sisters, yes, and even his own life" (Luke 14:26) cannot be his disciple. "Whoever does not bear his own cross and come after me, cannot be my disciple" (Luke 14:27), he said, and added, ". . . whoever of you does not renounce all that he has cannot be my disciple" (Luke 14:33). He makes demands! It costs something to be a disciple of Jesus Christ.

Both as individuals and as churches, Christian laymen are called upon to sacrifice. They must speak the word that needs to be spoken, though half the members of their church resign in protest. For Christ's sake, they must risk losing a friendship, a job, or their social standing. They may be called upon to risk indebtedness and mortgage their buildings for the sake of the gospel. It may not be visible to the naked eye, but wherever they go, they will be carrying some cross. A disciple pays a heavy price.

A disciple is also one who speaks his Master's mind. That is different from speaking his own mind. There are already too many uninhibited people spouting evil as though it were gospel and doing it on the grounds that there is something inherently good about saying what they think. That isn't so. We are to preach the *gospel,* and we are to do it without hesitation.

And we are to do it in love. That's another characteristic of a disciple. He has a special relationship to others. "By this all men will know that you are my disciples," Jesus said, "if you have love for one another" (John 13:35).

Most Christians try to love their fellowman. They work

hard to keep their church a congenial fellowship, but much of that goodwill is on the surface. Let laymen divide over loyalty to their minister, and watch the flames flare. Let a difference of opinion emerge with regard to a social issue, and see what prejudice, fear, and even hatred have been silently thriving beneath that cover of congeniality. I don't like to criticize the church, for I love it. It is painful to me to point to its mistakes. But its existence is at stake, and this is no time to dodge facts. The truth is that sometimes the fellowship is so superficial that every debate endangers it, and one person's hurt pride is enough to tear it apart. Let us not deceive ourselves. The church is not yet the loving fellowship that it is meant to be. That is because we have not yet learned to be disciples. Not membership, but discipleship is to be recognized by its loving relationships.

There are several other discernible aims in the religious revolution, but I am going to call your attention to just one more. It is the shift from *amorality to a morality.* In matters of human decency, the layman who would qualify as a revolutionist must get out of the sand and stand on a rock.

If you ask what moral and ethical issues we are talking about, the answer is all of them. Any question of right and wrong, bad and worse, good and better is a moral question. However, when we talk about the moral crisis in our nation, our thinking begins to focus on such particulars as our changing sex attitudes, the rising crime rate, dishonesty in business and government, the rights of minorities, and our widespread notion that anything is moral if you enjoy it and anything is ethical if you can get away with it.

There was a time when it was assumed that a good churchman was a representative of personal virtue. He was a man of integrity; his word could be trusted. He was chaste; he had respect both for himself and others. He was sober—not with regard to alcohol alone, but in connection with every human appetite. And he was loyal; belonging to a church, he was true to it; affirming a faith, he was faithful.

I would not infer that there are no churchmen like that today. Neither would I so romanticize the past as to suppose that the churches of an earlier generation harbored no faithlessness. But I do affirm that many of our forefathers lived by stricter codes than we. They were not always righteous, but they had a well-developed sense of sin. They often fell short of their ideals, but they had no question about what their ideals were.

By contrast, most modern churchmen are vague about their moral standards. Their convictions have been fading until it is increasingly difficult to distinguish them from the gray uncertainty of society in general. Most of them either avoid the subject of morality altogether, talk about it in a confused and contradictory manner, or boldly defend their deviations from Christian uprightness as realistic and therefore Christian.

J. Robert Moskin, senior editor of *Look* magazine, says that "the great majority of Americans, who want to try to live moral lives, no longer can be certain what is right and what is wrong." Governor George Romney of Michigan claims that the general decline in our moral character "is more serious to our future than the external threats we face." And Professor Chris Argyris of Yale says, "At the moment we have a world that has the cards stacked against the morally behaving man."

Our moral decay is far advanced. Presumably responsible people, meticulously honest in dealings with individuals, blandly cheat large corporations. Insurance clients claim injuries they do not have, and brokers can be found to encourage them in the deception. Policemen in large cities sometimes raid stores at night; guests fleece hotels of silverware, towels, finger bowls, and even Bibles; and customers and employees unite in robbing the nation's business establishments of millions of dollars worth of merchandise annually. Stolen shopping carts alone show up on the books of supermarkets as an annual fifteen million dollar loss. And in spite of the law of the land, many people, a disproportionate number of them churchmen, continue to force Negroes into ghettos, denying them the simple dignity of basic human rights.

Meanwhile, the topless bathing suit measures the fallen sex standards. Sophomoric adults treat sex like a handshake, while youth are set adrift on a sea more dangerous than anyone has bothered to tell them. From movies, magazines, and TV programs—their most dedicated teachers—they learn that to suppress their sexual urges is the great sin and to express them fully is to find life's ultimate meaning. Dr. Robert Fitch, Dean and Professor of Christian Ethics, sums the situation up when he says, "No previous generation of young people has had such an enormous and detailed amount of information made available to it concerning the scientific facts. And probably none has been left so ignorant of and so undisciplined in the ethical essentials."

This is not a defense of stern and rigid moralism. An angry father disinheriting a son whose waywardness has smirched the family name is not the picture of righteousness but bigotry. And the spectacle of the protected and untempted person heaping shame upon the frightened one who fought a losing battle with temptation is no model of Christian behavior. Nevertheless, the alternative to such misguided moralism ought to be something more constructive than moral nihilism and ethical anarchy.

But the distressing fact is that, confronted with the present decadence, the Christian church seems helpless to come up with that better alternative. Samuel H. Miller, Dean of the Harvard Divinity School, says that the most it has to offer "people living in a desperate age" is a place in which "to tranquilize their disturbing experiences—like some kind of lullaby."

Part of the problem is with our preachers. When prophetic utterance on moral issues is needed, too many of their tongues are tied. Moskin says that "the realtor and banker wield greater power over morality than the minister." J. Irwin Miller, manufacturer, speaking of some moral or ethical dilemma a businessman may face, says, "You take this problem to your preacher, and he takes to the hills." This problem was discussed recently at a seminar of ministers and businessmen at Harvard. The businessmen agreed that they all confronted the necessity of making major ethical decisions in their work. They also agreed that the ministers of their acquaintance were of no help to them in making those decisions. The best these men of the cloth could do, they said, was to offer the helpful advice that prayerful consideration be given to the matter.

There is no doubt that the pulpit's voice on moral matters has been weak. This is due in part to a sentimental view of morality, part to guilty involvement in immorality, and part to cowardice and confusion.

But another factor may be the crucial one in reducing the church's moral thunder to a helpless sigh: there is no longer a unity of moral conviction among church members. The church cannot speak persuasively with a cracked voice.

Of course, complete unity of moral conviction in the church is neither likely nor desirable. But the careful nurture of a mature Christian conscience is a responsibility we have been neglecting. The revolution in the church calls for a revival of it. We shall not always agree on what the Christian position is with regard to specific issues, but there should be no cause for debate about the church's responsibility for lifting moral standards and correcting ethical deficiencies.

Nevertheless, there are wide differences of opinion on these matters whether they are ever openly debated or not. Introduce a really tense ethical or messy moral problem to an average group of laymen and see what a variety of responses is stimulated.

Some of them will react with shocked helplessness. They are too far removed from the world's temptations to have a feeling for what is happening. They live a protected life. For them, immorality is a foreign country they have never visited. All they can do is read shocking reports about it and cluck their dismay.

Another group will lapse into guilty silence. They have compromised so many of their standards that they have lost their moral authority. They find it expedient to keep silent, lest their private Pandora's box be opened.

Still others will react with moral rigidity. Meticulously careful about their own behavior, they have an unhealthy compulsion to clean up the rest of the world. They are legalistic, "judgmental," and possessed with an urge to punish. They are insensitive, hateful, and domineering. And some of them are at the same time disarmingly sweet little ladies who make the best pies for the potlucks, or those clean-cut looking men who make such gentlemanly ushers.

A fourth group of laymen are at the opposite pole. They are the ones who have schooled themselves to be shocked at nothing and to condemn no one. Always "understanding" the evil-doer and never "standing under" any strong moral conviction of their own, they are ready to forgive anything so as not to have a fuss. Eager to understand everybody's point of view, they are themselves without conviction. Through gradual accommodation to subchristian standards, these churchmen have lost their Christianity without knowing it. They have erased the line between right and wrong so many times, to move it over, that the whole area has grown smudgy and they no longer know where the line is.

Then there is that group of laymen whose sense of right and wrong is strong but whose knowledge of Christian ethics is weak. Their moral judgments are based on political loyalties or the economic theories that work to their advantage. The standards that are really important to them are the standards of their social set. They are more interested in interpreting the Christian faith in such a manner as to support their way of living than to adjust their way of living to the standards of the Christian faith.

Fortunately there are other laymen who fall into none

of the above categories. These are the ones who study the Christian faith with understanding and apply its ethics with wisdom and dedication. They have the realism to see the world as it is and the idealism to know it can be better. Our hope rests in them. Unity of moral conviction among church members is not likely in our generation, if ever. Nevertheless, the church includes many responsible individuals whose religious insights are sound and whose actions are characterized by integrity and high purpose. They can be depended upon to seek the cooperation of others in doing right. When the cooperation is given, they are thankful for the strength it adds to their moral stand. When it is withheld, they remain true to their ideals without cursing the church as a whole for not sharing them. This is the only realistic and mature approach to the problem.

There is a revolution going on in the world and in the church. However, as serious and as far-reaching as it is, it need not alarm the Christian unduly, for out of the turmoil of our time a new kind of church is emerging. No one knows exactly what it will be like, but the bare outline of its structure is beginning to appear. If I see accurately what is coming, the change will be a shift from sham to integrity. In the new day, we shall not talk about worship and then talk during worship; we shall stop talking, and worship! We shall not claim to be disciples and then be content with our names on a membership roll; we shall forsake all and follow Jesus Christ! We shall not hold up high standards and then walk away from them; we shall do our best to go and sin no more!

II

The Dignity of Being a Layman

Revolutions upset dignity. They overturn established value systems and bring embarrassment to many. The revolution in the church has already proved unnerving to those whose churchmanship was insecure. In the hope of helping to keep such casualties at a minimum, we turn our attention to the problem of human dignity as it relates to the Christian layman. He must not let the present turmoil destroy his sense of significance.

Actually, subtle forces of deterioration have been at work for some time so that the layman's self-confidence has already been corroded. However, counter forces of reconstruction are also at work. The tug of these negative and positive tensions will show up in this chapter.

We begin by noting that church membership has little meaning for modern man. There are exceptions of course, but on the whole those who have joined the church have weak ties to it and those who have not joined are unimpressed by it.

The San Francisco Chronicle's "Question Man" found this to be true when he appeared on Stinson Beach one Sunday morning to ask the Sabbath sun bathers why people go to church. Although some had religious backgrounds, none took the church seriously. One said he had learned in college that there were better things to do on Sunday than go to church. Another valued the church only as a pleasant place "to relax and think in peace," and a third conceded that church attendance "makes you feel better" so that your "soul rests easier for the following week of sin." One said that church people are blind followers of folkways and another referred to church attendance as "a crutch."

As fas as I know, Vance Packard was not among those questioned that Sunday morning, but his sociological findings confirm the answers that were given. He says that for most American Christians "going to church is the nice thing that proper people do on Sundays. It advertises their respectability, gives them a warm feeling that they are behaving in a way their God-fearing ancestors would approve, and adds (they hope) a few cubits to their social stature by throwing them with a social group with which they wish to be identified." He is certain that today more people choose a particular church for social or business reasons than for doctrinal reasons. I do not know if this is true. But I am sure that many church members are as superficial in their acceptance of the church as the Stinson Beach crowd were in their rejection of it. Certainly the record of most of those who have taken vows of church membership is not impressive. Many of them never attend Sunday worship services and a large proportion of those who do, attend irregularly. An embarrassingly large number of persons whose names are on church rolls make no financial contributions, and an even larger percentage do no church work of any kind. As for the fundamental Christian task of winning others to the faith, a large majority have done nothing. For a growing number of laymen, church membership is a loose harness which is accepted lightly and shed easily. Seldom is it buckled to a significant load. There is something, perhaps a superstition, that prevents most people with a Christian heritage from throwing the church over completely, but it is not often the dominant influence in their lives.

The perceptive writer, Joseph Wood Krutch, has expressed the opinion that many people, accepting the invitation to "Attend the Church of Your Choice," look for one that will confirm their prejudices rather than refine and toughen their beliefs. If the church they go to disturbs them, it obviously is not "the church of their choice," so they must logically choose another. Their church, like their cigarette, is successful if it soothes. If they are not satisfied, they switch. So superficial has church membership become in the lives of many that they attend Sunday services only because they find it mildly pleasant, or at least less painful than having to justify their absence to their conscience or family.

There are many reasons for this widespread superficiality. One is the age of the church. We have been in business a long time, and like any organization that has outlived the generation that spawned it, we are in danger of becoming an anachronism, irrelevant, and attracting only the superficial. Another reason is to be found in the uninspired lives of our most faithful adherents. Burdened with the chores of church dinners or perpetually gloomy from poring over church budgets that fail to balance, they advertise the notion that the church is more of a worry than a wonder.

In addition to this, many church members downgrade their own status. They often introduce themselves by saying, "I am just a layman," inferring a station inferior to that of the minister and suggesting that being a layman is of secondary significance. They have little sense of the inherent dignity of belonging to the company of God. Some of them are conscientious, hard-working and dedicated; some are merely sentimental; others are so casual about the church as to be flippant. But nearly all of them lack something important that earlier Christians possessed. They lack a whole-souled belief in the church. They lack the unspeakable joy of being disciples of Christ. They lack the dignity that does not come with title or position and is not found in physical bearing and social graces but is the natural state of those possessed by a passion to serve the Lord of the Universe.

The New Testament church had this. J. B. Phillips refers to it as "the Church as it was meant to be." He calls it "vigorous and flexible," existing as it did in "the days before it ever became fat and short of breath through prosperity, or muscle-bound by over-organization." Speaking of the laymen of this early church, he says, "These men did not make 'acts of faith,' they believed; they did not 'say their prayers,' they really prayed. They did not hold conferences on psychosomatic medicine, they simply healed the sick." Referring to "the glory of the Church in the early age of the Apostles," Samuel H. Miller says:

> It is true that they had no great buildings. They met in synagogues. They met in Roman basilicas. They met in all kinds of hand-me-down places. They met in houses and homes and even in jails; but that was a great Church! . . . They did not care whether they were dispossessed or not. They did not care whether they were respectable or not. They had something that the world had never given them. They did not care whether they had churches or not. They did not care, in a sense, whether they lived or not. They were arrested, thrown into jails, martyred; they were persecuted, hounded, shamed and disgraced. All the while they sang their Te Deums and testified: "This thing that we have is more valuable than anything we ever knew. We would not exchange it for wealth or respectability or prestige. We will die first."[1]

That's true Christian commitment, but it scarcely describes a majority of today's church members. Maybe it

[1] *The Life of the Church* (New York: Harper & Row, 1953), p. 12.

shouldn't. Yet, I have an idea that today's laymen are homesick for something the apostles had. They long for a meaningful church experience but don't know how to get it. They hunger for a religious life that satisfies and grow restless when the church to which they belong fails to produce it. To be sure, they are invited to "get active"—to serve on key committees and to participate in fellowship groups. But this isn't exactly what they are looking for. They have no objection to organization. Committee work needs to be done. They are willing to grant this. They know that the church must have their financial support if it is to keep its doors open, and they want it to stay in business. But only a few get any real satisfaction out of their church. The rest remain faithful through fear disguised as duty or silently slip away.

What has gone wrong? To join the Christian church is the greatest thing that one can do. It is to set one's life in its God-intended course. It is to become a part of the redeeming fellowship of Jesus Christ. It is to engage in the most worth-while ventures it is given man to perform. It is to say "yes" to God's call. How then has churchmanship become for so many a bore, a nuisance, a frustration, a disappointment?

There are many factors involved. One is that most church members have lost their self-confidence. They have forgotten the dignity of being laymen. Dignity means "worthiness; nobility." It involves knowing one's *worth* (Christ died for him), and one's royal blood (he is a child of God). With this knowledge the churchman stands tall; without it he cowers. With it he carries confidence; without it he is insecure. This is true regardless of outward circumstances. That is why so often in history, churchmen in jail have shown themselves to be freer than their jailers; churchmen under persecution prove to be stronger than their oppressors; and churchmen in humiliating circumstances are less embarrassed than those who have sought to humiliate them. There is great dignity in being a churchman. It gives a man an awareness of his worth which is something that psychologists, too often without success, seek to arouse in their clients.

But how does one find it in churchmanship? What is the dignity of being a layman?

First of all there is the dignity of belonging to a worthy company. Everyone seeks a measure of distinction. He wants to belong to the "right" group. That's what the church is. Yet it has few of the earmarks popularly associated with groups at the top.

It does not cater to snobbishness. It does not aim its appeal to young executives, people who can afford the best, or adults with discriminating tastes.

It is not confined to people with certain intellectual capacities. College degrees do not figure in church membership.

There are no economic requirements. No one asks to know the assets of a prospective member.

Personal appearance has nothing to do with it. No one is kept out of church because he has a limited wardrobe or dresses in poor taste or forgets to comb his hair.

Race and nationality are not factors to be considered. Granted there are churches that draw the color line, just as there are churches that cater to certain social groups, but these practices are heretical. They do not represent the true church.

Family history or length of residence are immaterial to the Christian fellowship. To be sure, as the secular is constantly impinging on the religious, there are those who introduce these factors and refer to a young woman as coming from a "fine old church family" or describe a man as one who has been a member for fifty years. But these things are immaterial to the basic nature of the church. We have no "Native Sons" no "Daughters of the Christian Revelation."

The question naturally arises, "If none of the generally accepted symbols of status apply to membership in the church, what dignity is there in belonging to it?"

There is the dignity of rising above the need for the usual

symbols of status. There is the dignity of belonging to a fellowship that transcends all barriers. There is the dignity of participating in a venture that is eternal and following a Leader who is Spirit, Light, Love, Power, Truth, and who is concerned about his followers. If there is any greater dignity than this, I do not know of it.

National boundaries mean little to the church: throughout the bitter conflict of World War II, Christians in the warring countries retained their unity. Iron curtains cannot divide it: in Soviet and American spheres of influence, Christians worship the same God. Time does not wear it away: as Daniel Jenkins puts it, in *The Strangeness of the Church:* "In the perspective of history, the Church stands out as the most remarkable institution or group of institutions the world has ever seen. . . . It has persisted as a strong and effective focus of men's loyalty longer than any nation which is prominent in the modern world." Social and educational differences cannot shake us apart: the church is the true "classless society" where "There is neither Jew nor Greek, there is neither slave nor free, there is neither male nor female; for you are all one in Christ Jesus" (Gal. 3:28). Even death fails to sever the body of the church: we are still united with those whom we have "loved long since and lost a while." We experience the communion of saints. We are led by a crucified and risen Lord. That great hymn of the church is right about it: "We are not divided, All one body we . . ."

The second thing that gives dignity to being a layman is belonging to a loving fellowship.

Jesus considered his followers to be a brotherhood, welded together through the bonds of love. "A new commandment I give to you, that you love one another . . . By this all men will know that you are my disciples, if you have love for one another" (John 13:34–35). The disciples picked up this concept and the brotherhood became all-important. They were the family of God, their church was the household of faith, and they called each other "brethren."

". . . Love the brotherhood . . ." (I Pet. 2:17), counseled Peter, and John reminded the members of the early church that "He who loves his brother abides in the light . . ." (I John 2:10).

This close filial feeling among church members was evident in our grandfather's day. It was expressed in their frequent singing of such songs as "Blest Be the Tie That Binds." Believers singing,

> We share each other's woes,
> Each other's burdens bear,
> And often for each other flows
> The sympathizing tear.

had little reason to mumble the current complaint of disconnected people whining that they are not loved or understood, or cared for. Belonging to the church, they knew they were loved.

In his book, *Herein Is Love*, Reuel L. Howe says that "our deepest need is to be loved," but that we do not find love by running around looking for it. We find it by loving. "And when we find love by loving, we find God." The church is a focal point of love of God for man, and man for God, and man for man. In this fellowship each individual is strengthened when he is weak, and when he is strong, his strength supports others.

Nowhere have I seen the concept of the church as a loving fellowship more dramatically illustrated than in Ernest Gordon's *Through the Valley of the Kwai.*[2] The book is the story of his experience as a prisoner of the Japanese during World War II. In the presence of despair, forced labor, disease, starvation, and naked brutality, says Gordon, "Existence had become so miserable, the odds so heavy against us, that nothing mattered except to survive. We lived by the rule of the jungle, 'red in tooth and claw'—the evolutionary law of the survival of the fittest. It was a case of 'I look out for myself and to hell with

[2] New York: Harper & Row, 1962, pp. 74 ff.

everyone else.' . . . The weak were trampled underfoot, the sick ignored or resented, the dead forgotten.

"Hate, for some, was the only motivation for living," he said. "We hated the Japanese. We would willingly have torn them limb from limb, flesh from flesh, had they fallen into our hands. In time even hate died, giving way to numb, black despair . . . We had no church, no chaplains, no services. If there were men who kept faith alive in their hearts they gave no sign."

Then something happened to these prisoners. They were transformed—literally, completely and unbelievably transformed! Their basic environment remained the same. All of the factors that had reduced them to selfishness, hate, and despair were still present, but the selfishness, hate, and despair were lifted from them. It is difficult to tell exactly how it happened. The subtle, imperceptible movement of the Spirit cannot always be traced with accuracy. But it happened.

Says Gordon, "Death was still with us—no doubt about that. But we were being slowly freed from its destructive grip." The sick were no longer ignored until they died, but with tenderness like a mother's, were nursed back to health when this was possible, and comforted through faith when death was inevitable. There was a new eagerness for learning. Amputees had artificial limbs made for them, ingeniously created from what materials the men could find in camp or in the adjoining jungle. New prisoners, arriving in a mood of hopelessness and despair, found themselves loved and cared for by their fellow prisoners. At first they were bewildered by this unexpected kindness, and then transformed.

When the Japanese were finally defeated and victorious allies came into the prison camp, the angered liberators were ready to slaughter the guards. "Only the intervention of the victims prevented them. Captors were spared by their captives. 'Not an eye for an eye, a limb for a limb this time,' said these exhausted but forgiving men."

What had happened to these men? The answer is as

simple as it is dramatic. *They became the church* and experienced the power of its loving fellowship. Of course they did not become a church in the traditional sense. They became the church in the true sense, nevertheless.

Perhaps it all began when Angus McGillivray died of starvation after nursing his pal to health by sharing portions of his own meager food ration with him, sleeping in the cold in order to make his blanket available to his sick friend, and risking his own life by sneaking out of camp to barter for medicine.

Hearing this story of loving sacrifice, and others like it, the men began to extract from the remote corners of their minds, where they had placed things they thought were obsolete, sayings like this: "Greater love has no man than this, that a man lay down his life for his friends" (John 15:13). No doubt some remembered more: "This is my commandment, that you love one another as I have loved you" (John 15:12). The men began, cautiously at first, to say to one another that such behavior made sense. Presently they were meeting in little groups to study the Bible. An altar and a place of worship were created and church services were held regularly. In due course these prisoners-turned-churchmen turned their death camp into a place of spiritual triumph. The prisoners developed a quiet dignity their oppressors did not know, for they had joined the company of those who care.

A third thing that gives dignity to being a layman is belonging to a fellowship that allows a man to be himself.

Much of the time we are forced to play a role—at least we think we are. We get caught up in the game of projecting the right "image." This is a switch from the day in which our concern was for a man's character, not his image, and we gave ourselves to a vocation, not a role.

The words "image" and "role" both suggest sham. An image is an imitation of something, not the real thing. And a role is a part one plays, a character one must slip out of, if he is to be his real self. All of this suggests that we are a generation of pretenders, more concerned about what we appear to be than what we are. Not sure of our identity, we are prone to select a "role" that looks interesting and then concentrate on doing a good job of acting. This is unfortunate. We would be better off if we would quit assuming roles and start being persons.

Everyone longs for integrity. He wants to be real. Pretense makes him lonely. He may seek status but he doesn't really want it. He wants selfhood. I know that because I've watched the barriers go down between myself and others when I am most honest about my own desires, doubts, fears, and aspirations. When I express a phony ideal, usually accompanied by a few words that can be identified as "spiritual," I get a phony reaction. *My* pretense meets the *other fellow's.* With this superficial exchange we smile and nod approvingly as a way of assuring one another we are playing our roles as expected, but we had better not try to break through the wall to the real person. Too many conversations between ministers and laymen fall into this category and have no more human value than an interchange of ideas between a couple of tape recorders. Anyone with an ounce of integrity is sickened even to hear it, to say nothing of participating in it. It's a commendable thing to affirm a spiritual truth, but an honest confession of doubt, resentment, anger, lust, or fear has more power to convert a sinner any day than a dishonest affirmation of faith. It has more power just because it is honest. And maybe, also because it is courageous.

Another reason I know that people want integrity is because I want it and I am a person. I hate being around people who force me to pretend. I resent *them* for what they make me do, and I resent *myself* for doing it. Some people won't accept me when I'm honest. It is more important to them for me to fit their image of a minister than that I be true to myself. They can't accept my prayer "God, be merciful to me a sinner" (Luke 18:13) unless they can be sure I am just quoting. Even if I try to convince them the prayer is for me, they will seek to soften my painful confession by using it as evidence of my humility. They won't let me be sinful, not because I am not but because they can't stand the shattering of their ministerial image. And they won't let me be controversial. They won't actually insist that my ideas on politics and culture correspond with theirs, but if they differ, they will thank me to keep my ideas to myself and let no remark of mine disturb the serenity of our relationship.

I resent this kind of imprisonment. I despise the forces that conspire to make me something I am not. If I despise them, others must also. Surely every human being longs for the freedom to be honestly and completely himself.

The church provides this. It accepts people as they are. There is dignity in this. An association of people who have learned to face themselves and others honestly is as strong as truth. It has moved past any embarrassment in approaching the altar of God singing:

> Just as I am, though tossed about
> With many a conflict, many a doubt,
> Fightings and fears within, without,
> O Lamb of God, I come, I come!

Always there is the assurance that ". . . him who comes to me I will not cast out" (John 6:37). In the fellowship of the church a man can afford to be himself.

We have said so far that the layman finds personal dignity in belonging to the church because it is a fellowship that is above making social distinctions, a fellowship that surrounds its members with loving concern, and a fellowship that allows a man to be himself. Note also that there is dignity in it because it is a fellowship committed to no lesser purpose than serving the Lord of the universe.

Its heroes are men who obey God rather than man. There is something grand about those mighty men of the Old Testament, defying kings and empires as they boldly chose to do the will of Jehovah. One's heart beats a little faster as he reads again of the courageous "Acts of the Apostles," those men who would rather die than disobey a single command from God. And what churchman can cease to wonder at the youthful Jesus, risking everything on what Santayana calls "the soul's invincible surmise," but what Jesus called "truth." His garden prayer, ". . . not as I will, but as thou wilt" (Matt. 26:39), sets the single guiding principle for every churchman.

We are told that ours is a generation of people for whom life has little meaning. This is true I am sure. Everywhere you can find people looking for goals, seeking some purpose, and failing in the search, reduced to busy-work to divert their minds from their emptiness. In the church it is different. No one genuinely committed to serving the God of the universe every moment of every day will be melted down to boredom or driven to desperation. Historian Arnold Toynbee has said: "Man at work can be happy and spiritually healthy only if he feels that he is working in God's world and for God's glory through doing what is God's work." Churchmen find that happiness and spiritual health, for they are dedicated to the single purpose of "doing what is God's work." There is dignity in that.

Let's face another set of facts. Over against the true character of the church we must place the modern caricature of it. In its pure form, the church is worthy, loving, accepting, and completely devoted to God as we have said. The average American church member, however, has little feeling for this high character of the church. Absorbed in balancing the budgets, staffing the church school, and planning meetings, he needs to know that a church is not well administered just because it operates efficiently. It is well administered only if it accomplishes what a church is meant to accomplish. When John sent his disciple to ask Jesus if he were ". . . he who is to come . . ." (Matt. 11:3), Jesus didn't answer, "Tell John I have selected twelve disciples and they are all assigned to one of the six commissions.

We have surveyed the neighborhood and plan to build within six months." He said, "Go and tell John what you hear and see: the blind receive their sight and the lame walk, lepers are cleansed and the deaf hear, and the dead are raised up, and the poor have good news preached to them" (Matt. 11:4–5). He was doing what the Messiah was supposed to do. That was his badge of authenticity.

The same test must be put to the church. Take the concept of the church as a brotherhood, for example. This idea has been watered down in recent years until church members actually feel less loving loyalty toward one another than is found among fraternity brothers or the members of a lodge. There may be a few laymen who think of their fellow church members as their family, but there aren't many. In part this is due to the increased mobility of the population. People join a church and are gone again before anyone comes to know them. It is also true that whereas people used to give all their time to the church, they now divide it among numerous worthy community endeavors. This means they develop pleasant working relationships with more people and deep bonds of loyalty to fewer. Their church friends lose their special relationship with them and become little more than acquaintances. There is a possibility that churchmen have become so obsessed with the brotherhood of all men that they have failed to develop the brotherhood of that group of men who form the church. In their fear of becoming exclusive, they have extended themselves to the point where they no longer have much to include anybody in.

If the church is to survive with power for our generation it must once again become a warm and effective brotherhood. When a member is sick, let no layman think he has discharged his responsibility when he has notified the church office. Let him call on the sick brother himself, offering what service he can render. He should do more than report the presence of a stranger in the church; he should befriend him. Troubled members should receive his encouragement; the bereaved should feel his support; the poor should receive his financial assistance. When someone in the community is in need, every layman should feel free to offer service in the name of his church as the brotherhood reaches outward. As Dr. Tom Dooley used to accompany each bit of relief he offered the people of Laos with the simple words, "This is American aid," every layman should extend help to nonchurchmen in the spirit and in the name of the Christian fellowship.

Consider the "accepting" nature of the church, its readiness to let a man be his true self. Here again we are forced to admit that many churches in America do not provide that kind of environment at all. Perhaps this is the great peril of the modern church. Too many of its members are charlatans. Their religion is a façade, and there are still enough people around who are close enough to reality to spot the deception. They know that if a churchman preaches brotherhood and practices segregation, he is a fake. If he uses the cross as a symbol but never gives to the point of sacrifice, he is a fake. If he declares his allegiance to the Golden Rule and withholds food from starving Chinese, he is a fake. If he "accepts Christ as his personal Savior" and is so insecure he can't allow his church or minister to dive into controversial issues, he is a fake. If, in the name of the Christ who died for all men, he is active in a one-class suburban church made up of a lot of people with cultural values like his own, and he does nothing to develop meaningful relationships with other kinds of people, he is a fake. If today's church is to be the true church, it has a long way to go in this area of accepting people, and encouraging them to accept themselves, just as they are.

The idea that the church is a group of people wholly committed to serve God, must submit to a loose interpretation if it is to apply to today's churchmen. Most of them are uncertain and half committed. They don't serve God with conviction because they aren't certain what he wants them to do. In fact, they aren't even sure he exists!

It's a ludicrous situation when you stop to look at it. Here we are, the mighty church of God, declaring ourselves to be the body of Christ, the source of the world's salvation, the fellowship of believers, the company of the committed, prophets, soldiers of Christ, bearers of Good News. We build mighty cathedrals and thrust their cross-topped towers into the sky! Then we gather inside in timid little groups and ask each other, "What is the mission of the church?" Or we get on the phone and round up our members to get them to an important meeting which begins impressively with lusty singing about the survival power of our fathers' faith "in spite of dungeon, fire and sword," and ends by postponing for another month the decision as to whether to cut the budget or let the custodian go. Or we attract the youth with ping-pong and volleyball, social dances and night-club lighting, and finally assembling them for "the serious part of our program," scratch at the surface of their rapidly hardening boredom by asking them, "What would you like to talk about?" Someone says, "Girls!" The uneasy titter and succession of silly remarks that follow convince the slightly psychologically oriented leader that sex is the area of their real concern. With the confidence that he is "meeting their real needs," he schedules a series of meetings on the subject, and feels deliciously daring. Or we sit, just two of us, in the minister's study, beautifully furnished for the most congenial counseling atmosphere. From one of us comes the invitation, "Now, tell me about your problem," and from the other, "Well, Doctor, I just don't know where to begin."

And that's about the problem we all face. We don't know where to begin—for the simple reason that we have retreated from the center, and at the periphery there are too many choices. The heart is single, and complications multiply in direct ratio to our distance from it.

Out on the edge we have become entangled in the superficial. We who are commissioned to bring men the great gift of God's love have settled for peddling gift wrappings.

Instead of making the gospel vital, we seek to make it attractive. Modern church architecture is designed to catch the eye. Spacious, well-equipped rooms are supposed to teach the children that religion is important. Friendly greeters at the door are there to make the stranger feel welcome. Well-oiled visitation schemes increase attendance and lift the level of giving. Addressograph plates take individual mailings to every member; robotypers make a thousand letters look individually typed and deceptively personal; and the mimeograph rises to the status of the holy roller. It just doesn't seem to get through to us that it is possible for a man to receive a friendly greeting at the door, worship in a strikingly beautiful sanctuary, attend Sunday school in a pleasingly decorated and air-conditioned room, receive a friendly letter from the pastor, and a well-meaning visit from laymen without ever getting the faintest hint of what the Gospel of Jesus Christ is all about. We are a generation that knows the tricks of the trade but not the trade.

Now see what happens. Having retreated from the heart of things, we have lost sight of the essentials. This leaves us frustrated and uneasy, vaguely, and sometimes acutely, feeling that something is missing. If we are ministers, we begin to doubt our calling and wonder if we should go into something else; we resent the authority of our ecclesiastical leaders, the criticisms that come from laymen, the relatively low economic base on which our family is forced to live, and the constant demands on our time. If we are laymen, we get tired of so much involvement and dialogue and communication and the existential situation. We weary of being told what our duty is, and of the burden of guilt we feel because we don't give more, help with more dinners, teach more Sunday-school classes, or take better care of our preacher. In short, we are all suffering from the disillusionment that comes from substituting peripheral matters for central matters.

Lonely and lost, away from the heart of the gospel, we catch hold of fragments on the outskirts and treat them as though they were the heart. In the science building at the Seattle World's Fair young monkeys were shown in a cage with no mother to relate to but a monkey-shaped bundle of wire. When frightened they would run and embrace this ridiculously inadequate mother substitute as a source of security. But the substitute failed to meet the young monkeys' real needs and they developed serious personality defects. That is something of what has happened to us. As a substitute for knowing and loving and serving God, we have turned to budgeting, record keeping, public relations, entertaining, food serving, architecture, and the group process. Our mistake is not in giving attention to these things. They all deserve attention. Our mistake is in giving central or exclusive attention to them. Like the monkeys' synthetic mother, they do not ultimately satisfy.

So we go after our crowds and raise money to meet the budget, which, if judged in terms of the time and effort put into it, has become the central mission of the church. Yet instinctively we know that there is something wrong with this. It was not to this we were called. So in disillusionment and frustration, laymen fall away from the church and ministers seek other employment more rapidly than we can replace them.

The problem is critical. Reuel L. Howe says: "The conversations of church members often are pitiful in their concern for the trivial affairs of the local church and institution, about its building and organizations, its suppers and bazaars. What a pathetic and inconsequential way of serving Christ!" And author Milton Mayer, returning to this country after visiting the hard-pressed churches of Eastern Europe where to make a Christian witness costs something, comments that he has the impression that in American churches the question of what to do about the floor in the Sunday-school gym is as great a concern as any they have.

Georgia Harkness sees the situation clearly when she writes of all the complicated organizational activities of the modern church as it involves itself with property, staff, educational programs, and social services, and concludes: "These institutional aspects of a church are for the most part necessary, and in spite of the perversions to which all sinful humanity is subject, they are for the most part good. Yet they are not primary, and their badness when this occurs stems mainly from what is rightfully secondary being made primary."

But calling churchmen to a nobler purpose, Dr. Harkness continues:

> As a fellowship of the followers of Christ, a church has one overarching function which transcends all others, and every particular function finds its criterion of usefulness in relation to it. The Church exists to be the carrier of the gospel of Christ; a church is, or it is not, in a full sense a church to the degree that its members are faithful to this mission. When it fails in this the people may meet in ever so grand and impressive a church building, they may have ever so good a time in each other's company, they may do ever so many fine things that are worth doing, but they are not really a church. Instead, they are a social gathering of congenial and usually rather nice people who for reasons of family connection or habit or the following of prevailing pattern—or even the hope of prestige as a factor in economic success—decide to stay with or unite with a church.[3]

The real churchman is the one who can say with Elisabeth Elliot, as she cut through all doubts and uncertainties as to whether or not she should go to live among the Auca Indians who had murdered her husband, "I knew one thing—I must obey God."

In this central commitment to serve God, the calling of

[3] *The Church and Its Laity* (Nashville: Abingdon Press, 1962), p. 87.

the layman and the calling of the minister are identical. It is not ordination that makes employment sacred. A minister who is more concerned with salary than with service and more eager for his church to make a good record in the denominational yearbook than an acceptable place in "the Lamb's book of life" (Rev. 21:27) is, in spite of his ordination, a thoroughgoing secularist. And the layman who goes about his work as engineer, salesman, or mechanic, determined to serve God through what he does, is fulfilling a calling to a sacred mission. He knows that in the church, membership means ministry. Jerome said it back in the fourth century: "Baptism is the ordination of the laity."

Paul addressed his letter to the Christians in the church at Rome: "To you all then, loved of God and *called to be Christ's men and women* . . ." (Phillips). Laymen, like ministers, are called by Christ to do his work. The very word "laymen" embodies this truth. It comes from the Greek word "laos" which means, "The people of God!"

Shortly after the assassination of President Kennedy, the British press is said to have reported that in her sorrow, Mrs. Kennedy gave the American people something they lacked: majesty! In that same way, we must bring to American churchmen something they have lost: dignity!—the sense of worth and nobility that rightfully belong to "the people of God."

III

Getting Oriented Theologically

Human dignity is not self-authenticating. It exists in relationship. In the case of the Christian layman it exists in relation to God. A person is "somebody" to the extent that he is "God's body"—that is, one through whom God can fulfill his will. Otherwise he is "nobody." Identity is found in deity. That is why theology is the most important concern of man.

The word "theology" scares people. They withdraw from it as they recoil from anything that seems big and mysterious. They think of the theologian as a mental giant who lives in a world they do not inhabit and speaks a language they do not understand.

There is some truth in this image. Religious intellectuals, like intellectuals in any other field can get carried away with themselves. The men at one theological seminary called a famous theologian who taught there by the nickname of "Peace" because, they said, he "passes all understanding" (Phil. 4:7).

There is a story about two cows looking at a milk truck which advertised milk that was "pasteurized, homogenized, standardized, Vitamin D added." One cow said to the other, "It makes you feel sort of inadequate, doesn't it?" That's the way some laymen feel when they compare their simple faith with the big terms the theologians toss around.

Failure to understand theological jargon, however, is slim evidence to prove one has a simple faith or an undeveloped theology. Impressive ecclesiastical verbiage can be used as a shield to hide one's spiritual poverty. Often it says more about one's inability to put great ideas into simple language than it says about God. On the other hand, people who have never learned to talk with that strange mixture of English, Latin, Greek, Hebrew, German, and newly coined words that are the theologian's trademark, may have great spiritual depth and understanding.

In some ways "theology" is an unfortunate word. When Jesus talked about God, he called him "Father" and made him as real to the Galilean peasants as the lilies and sparrows they saw about them. When we talk about God, our tendency is to move in the opposite direction. We turn academic and make him a subject to be studied in a course called "theology," required for students in graduate schools of religion. Jesus made complex truths simple without destroying them. We must be careful lest we make simple truths complex and thereby out of reach of the common man. Nevertheless, alert to the danger, we have no choice but to take the risk. We are not dealing with first-century Galilean peasants, but with twentieth-century Christian churchmen who are in no position to enjoy the luxury of too much religious simplicity. They should allow theology to lead them into a few paths they haven't bothered to travel.

Theology is a rigorous discipline. Anyone undertaking a serious study of it will be forced to think more deeply than he has before, and he will undergo the trauma of having some of his most cherished beliefs shattered. Perhaps this is the reason that the average layman tries to dodge it altogether. Most of us are about as eager to avoid mental and spiritual surgery as we are physical surgery. We want to grow in our religious ideas only if the process is not too disturbing.

The result of this mental cowardice has been ignorance, confusion, and a growing sense of meaninglessness. Ask the average churchman what difference a belief in immortality makes in his every day life. He doesn't know. It never occurred to him that there was any relationship. Ask him what bearing the cross of Christ has on the way he does his business. He'll answer, "Look. You're talking to the wrong man. I keep my business and religion in separate categories." Ask him why a prayer of confession appears in his church's order of worship. He'll shrug his shoulders and guess helplessly that it must be somebody's idea of a good program. Personally he thinks it is unnecessarily negative and he could get along very well without it. Ask him for the theological reasons he is registered with a particular political party. He'll look at you as if you were insane. What possible relationship could there be between one's religious beliefs and his political affiliations? The simple fact is that he has avoided any serious study of theology for so long that his religion has become detached from reality. It is a little like his appendix, acceptable enough so long as it doesn't give him trouble, but expendable when it hurts. The result has been the emergence in our churches of what has been called "religiosity." This means the continuance of religious forms following the disappearance of religious content. It is religion without reason.

That brings us to the meaning of theology. It has to do with the reasons. Theology is the study of God and of religion. A systematic theology is a carefully worked-out system of beliefs about essential things. Dr. Paul Tillich describes it as "that which concerns us ultimately."

Christians call this ultimate concern "God." He is the center of life around whom our existence revolves. He is the goal of life, toward which our existence moves. He is the ground of life, in which our existence is rooted. To know, to understand, and to act in accordance with this basic truth is the whole purpose of life.

Theology is not a department of life, confined to musty seminaries and a few people who happen to have a fascination for that sort of thing. It *is* life. It is not just one more area of inquiry to challenge the mind. It is the basic inquiry from which all other intellectual disciplines spring and to which they return when followed to the end. Physics, psychology, political science, sociology, and the rest are specialized fields. Theology embraces them all. It gives them unity and direction. Theology underlies all science, all government, all education, all society. When you get to the theological question, you get to the heart of the matter. And when you get to the heart of any subject you have struck theology.

To the knowledgeable Christian this is elementary. To most of today's churchmen it is incomprehensible. Their God is not at the center of life but on the periphery of it. He is on the periphery of their week, so they turn to him on Sunday. He is on the periphery of their vocation, so they forget him when they go to work. He is on the periphery of their minds, so they think of him only occasionally. He is on the periphery of their life in this world, so they think of death as the moment when at last they encounter him directly and associate with him constantly.

With God on the periphery, something else is at the center. It may be one's home or vocation or nation. It may be the pursuit of pleasure, the urge to succeed, or the desire to dominate. Whatever it is, if it is first and central, it has gained its position by crowding God out.

On one of my first dates with the girl who is now my wife, I asked her what she believed about God. Unaccustomed to this "line," she was startled at first, but came through well enough to qualify for another date. Meanwhile, she bought a book on basic beliefs, written by an author whom she knew I respected, and spent her spare time studying it in preparation for future encounters with unusual suitors. The next time we went out together I got around to theological considerations again, as she had anticipated that I would. "What do you believe about immortality?" I asked. With mingled charm and assurance, she came forth with a learned account of various positions and an intelligent declaration of her own. We were married soon after!

There is a line in the wedding ceremony which reads, "*If steadfastly you endeavor to do the will of your heavenly Father*,[1] your life will be full of joy, and the home which you are establishing will abide in peace." If the lovers' basic orientation is to God, their love will live and grow. If God is subordinate to their relationship with each other, the love that brought them to the altar will disintegrate when they leave it.

This truth can be expanded to include all of life's relationships: social, business, professional, national, international. If your central goal is to be popular, when the score is added up you will lose. If your central goal is to build a great business, in the last analysis you will fail. If your central goal is to establish a sovereign and independent nation, you are headed for disappointment. If your central goal is even so noble as world government and universal peace, your future holds disillusionment. But "if steadfastly you"—and your friends, and your business associates, and your fellow Americans, and your counterparts around the world—"endeavor to do the will of your heavenly Father, your life will be full of joy, and the home"—and the business and the nation and the world order—"you are establishing will abide in peace."

At any given moment, romance, business, or politics may seem more urgent than theology, but in the last analysis romance, business, and politics are meaningless if they are

[1] Italics mine.

not related to something bigger, something of ultimate concern. That which is not centered in God is of no use to man. Shakespeare put this conviction in the mouth of Cardinal Wolsey when he had him confess:

> Had I but served my God with half the zeal
> I served my king, he would not in mine age
> Have left me naked to mine enemies.

We are all left naked to our enemies when we leave theology to specialists and busy ourselves with other matters.

A lawyer friend of mine returned recently from a trip around the world. On his first day home, impressions of his tour still fresh in his mind, he reviewed his experiences in summary and perspective. This is the way he added them up: "I have returned convinced that in every nation, the major problems are theological. They stem from bad religion." How can India overcome famine and disease when its predominant religion perpetuates as holy the ritual of bathing in the "sacred" Ganges, though its waters are murky with human excrement and remains of the dead? How can Thailand face the dangers of a nuclear age with its people convinced that spirit houses ward off evil?

Whether "bad religion" expresses itself in African witch doctors treating disease with the practices of voodoo, Communist dictators substituting the state for God as the object of supreme devotion, Tibetan Buddhists spinning prayer wheels to make their prayers effective, Roman Catholics deifying relics, and using them as a means of invoking divine favor, or American Protestants defending segregation, spurning the demands of intellectual integrity, and offering divine sanction to political irresponsibility, bad religion underlies the world's evil.

The basic problem of both Fascism and Communism is that they are not rooted in a sound theology. They have virtues. No one can deny that. Mussolini got the trains running on time. Hitler inspired his people with new hope. The

Russian dictators brought a country from illiteracy to high standards of education. But something is wrong with all this. The motivation is wrong. Their belief about the nature and destiny of man is wrong. Their ideas about God are wrong. You can't start with a wrong idea about God and emerge with the good society.

Most Americans know this. What they do not know is that their reaction to these inadequate political philosophies shares equally in their own sin when that reaction has no sounder theological base. This is most apparent in America where some, through fear of the political right, become Communists while others, through fear of the political left, join the John Birch Society. Correctly, we lump these apparent opposites together and call them extremists. They are dangerous, a threat to society and, in this day of nuclear weapons, to all of life.

Like Fascists and Communists, these American extremists are the victims of bad religion. They have no rootage in eternal principles; no standards by which to measure competing philosophies; no understanding of ultimate things from which to approach all temporal things; no mature, responsible action—only reaction.

This is not to say they are unrelated to the Christian church. Many of them are church members, some of them even ministers. Not a few of them base their extremism on what they understand to be Christian doctrine. But they speak out of ignorance. In America as well as abroad, within Christianity as well as in other religions, the problem is a theological one.

If America has known greatness in the past and enjoys a measure of it now, it is because her founding fathers knew theology. They placed their trust in God. And if America loses its greatness, it will be because America loses its God. All governments need a clearer understanding of the nature and destiny of man, and the power and love of God. These are matters of theology. Indeed, the most frightening thing about our time is not Communism, or Fascism, or the threat of nuclear war, as disturbing as all these things are. The most frightening thing about our time is the shriveling up of the human soul, the terrible plight of educated people who can think and talk about nothing but themselves, the breakdown of a moral structure, the washing away of a spiritual foundation, the absence of goals that are greater than self-satisfaction, and the assertion of the right to waste one's life on superficialities if one happens to have a fancy for that sort of thing. Jesus said it best: "And do not fear those who kill the body but cannot kill the soul; rather fear him who can destroy both soul and body in hell" (Matt. 10:28).

Our tragedy is that submerged in the civil rights struggle and the Communist-capitalist struggle, we have lost sight of the eternal struggle between good and evil, darkness and light, heaven and hell. We are so eager to be relevant to the world that we are becoming irrelevant to God's purpose in the world. We are so busy watching what the United States, Russia, and China are doing that we have forgotten what God has done, through Christ, for us sinners. We are aware of our race, our nationality, our political affiliation, and our denomination, but unaware of our nature as sons of God and instruments of his redemptive power.

Does that sound old-fashioned to you? Perhaps it is. But it is old-fashioned truth. God in Christ is the center and the essence of all things. This simple fact is at the heart of Christian theology. The church exists for the purpose of directing the world to that center and assisting the world in partaking of that essence. This is our message and our mission.

All church activity should be related to that purpose. Too little of it is. Most members do not know that. Most of them just assume that anything done under the auspices of the church is *ipso facto* geared to the church's primary purpose. It isn't. The assumption is as irrational as to suppose that everything one eats is good for him.

Most of our churches are involved in all kinds of things which are unimportant because they are unrelated to our central purpose. Convinced that we should be concerned with the real problems people face, church groups discuss boy-and-girl relations, the race problem, the arms race, the United Nations, politics, Communism, alcoholism, and many other subjects of importance. We *should* discuss these things for the church that fails to do so has closed its eyes to life. But it does us no good to talk about any of these subjects if we have no firm theological base from which to operate. Many church groups have deteriorated into disorganized lecture platforms for anyone with a current enthusiasm. As church "groups" they may remain strong for some time, but sooner or later the perceptive observer identifies in them the inevitable emptiness of an almost purposeless organization in search of a diversion, some excuse for holding regular meetings. One of the worst things happening to ministers these days is their too ready acceptance of invitations to speak to such groups. With a buzz of busyness about them, they dash from group to group as program fillers, sanctified entertainers, convincing everybody that ministers are human and convincing nobody that God is great.

Program chairmen inviting a minister to speak should have a better reason for doing so than that they have a space to be filled in their year's program or that they want a "good speaker." There should even be a better reason than that each year the organization tries to pay its respects to organized religion by inviting a clergyman to appear before them. I'll tell you why they should ask him. They should ask him because they are lost without God, and they need some help in finding him. They should ask him because so much of life seems meaningless, and they need to be directed to the meaningful. They should ask him because it is so easy to get values confused, and they need to hear from someone who believes in integrity and purity, and unselfishness and love. They should ask him because the basic questions of life are theological questions and they had better face the basic questions.

As for the minister, he should steadfastly resist the image of the "popular speaker," the "successful administrator," the "faithful caller," and insist on being cast in the role he is called to play: a spokesman for the living God.

The problem is that *we have substituted involvement for direction.* Tired of the aimlessness of their lives, people turn to the church for help in finding a worthy purpose, and we respond by getting them "involved" in some church activity.

"Involvement" is one of the more recent additions to our vocabulary of sacrosanct verbiage. It seems to mean about the same as "fellowship," which was yesterday's rallying cry except that it implies deeper entanglement and a louder voice in the planning. It suggests that we were on the right road when we said that fellowship was what the church was for, but that we didn't go far enough.

The goal now is for involvement to lead us into "dialogue." For those who never heard of Socrates, this has the exciting ring of the latest thing. For devotees of the ancient philosopher it suggests participation in something with great intellectual overtones. In actual practice it seems to be about what my generation of youth meant by discussion groups or bull sessions, and what all sensible people do when they sit down to talk things over with folks from different backgrounds and with varying points of view.

So today, "involvement" in "dialogue" is the thing. This calls for "small face-to-face groups." These are little circles of people who are supposed to feel free to shoot because they can see the whites of one another's eyes. This is considered to be superior to hearing a well-prepared address delivered to a sizable audience by a man who knows what he is talking about. It is presumed to be an imposition on human rights to ask someone to listen if he isn't allowed to interrupt the speaker or to hear one man's point of view if he isn't given a chance to spout his own.

I am making sport of something a lot of people take seriously, I know. If it is upsetting to some, it may be because it is their sacred cow I am milking.

And I am ready to admit that there is some milk to be obtained. The theory behind the idea of "involvement" is that we learn and grow only as we are involved, which is sensible, and should be self-evident. Worship is significant as the worshiper submerges himself in the service of worship; ministers and laymen grow in grace as they enter meaningfully into one another's lives; and we discover the Christian faith as we practice it. This is sound psychology, sociology, and religion. It is what is meant by loving your neighbor, and bearing one another's burdens, and making it right with your brother, and being peacemakers, and spreading the gospel, and healing the brokenhearted, and a lot of other things that have been at the center of Christianity from the start. There is nothing new about the idea of involvement. It started with Eve.

It is the unprecedented emphasis on involvement for its own sake that forms our problem. That's why a reaction has set in. People are tired of talking without learning, working without accomplishing anything, cooperating in endeavors of small significance, and giving sacrificially for causes they do not understand. That is why the current cry is for *relevance* and *depth* and *meaning*.[2] Perhaps it is time to replace the word "involvement" with the word "direction." We must know where we are going, and waste time on nothing that does not take us closer to the goal.

This calls for major reform. As things stand today, most church groups have little or no sense of direction. They are isolated segments of something, but they don't know quite what. They are involved, but don't know why. Boards of trustees operate with business efficiency but in theological darkness. Members of finance committees know the tricks of salesmanship and the art of budgeting, but have never

[2] I interpret the popular use of these terms as indicative of a current need, which is probably what the use of the term "involvement" was at the beginning. But I regret the extent to which these recently popularized words, even such a rich one as "meaning" are becoming shibboleths used carelessly by unthinking people.

in their adult life read an intellectually challenging religious book. Woman's societies and adult Sunday-school classes follow the rule book and assemble for scheduled meetings, but are aware of no greater calling than to raise more money for something or other and get more people to join. Youth groups, made up largely of young people who have been exposed to the church's program of Christian education since they were born, have so little awareness of purpose that even regular participation hinges on the thin thread of some drafted counselor's capacity to hold their interest. Social action groups, which normally have at least some sense of the importance of the church's doing something for somebody, are often more highly stimulated by their political loyalties than their religious ones.

What is needed is for every layman to know why the church is in business. He should be so certain of the church's purpose that he never hesitates in stating it or wavers in his commitment to it. In attending the regular meeting of the board of trustees, his conscious aim should be to direct the powers of that organization toward fulfillment of God's call to his church. In evaluating the work of Christian education, his measuring stick should be the mission of the church. Every class and club, every board and committee, every fellowship group and study seminar that comes under the auspices of the church should have its sights locked securely and unmistakably on the church's central purpose. Involvement in church-sponsored activities is not enough. Laymen must learn to know the central purpose of the church and relate everything—every business decision, every social activity, every worship experience, every building program, every finance drive, every letter, phone call, and conversation—to it.

Clearly, theology is central. When we find the theological truth, we find the basic truth. But to say that theology is "central" and "basic" is not to say it is simple. Its inevitable complexity is what has given rise to the various streams of theological thought that ministers so often mention without explaining. It is difficult to categorize them or even to define them accurately, and a thorough review of them would be an extensive and complicated affair beyond the scope of this book. What we are interested in here is the broad outline of theological trends. The following simple analysis bears little resemblance to the careful and lengthy treatment these matters would be given in a textbook on theology. It is just a thumbnail sketch designed to assist the layman in finding his way through an ecclesiastical jungle.

Everybody is familiar with our great variety of denominations, and most people are confused by them. Ministers are often asked to define the differences between the denominations. This is difficult to do because the differences are not clear-cut. Often they are more historical than current, more theoretical than real. And frequently what differences exist are superficial, having nothing to do with the fundamentals.

Cutting across all denominations are certain theological trends. These streams of religious thought overflow denominational banks so that persons of different denominations often have more in common with each other than with persons of their own denomination who have a different theological bent. So what we are discussing here is not the different denominations, but a few of the different theological emphases which are most commonly referred to today.

One word of caution: although we are using labels for purposes of identification we must beware of labels. For clarification it is often useful procedure to categorize and label. But it is dangerous business to attach the label to anyone, since no individual quite fits the stereotype. Besides, these streams of theological thought are constantly intermingling. A "pure liberal," for example, is a "pure fiction." Such a person doesn't exist. All of these streams of theology are strongly conditioned by the inflowing of the other streams.

The first one is *fundamentalism.* The hard-core fundamentalist has a definite creed of rigidly stated beliefs from which there can be no deviation. He is convinced he is right and that his mission in the world is to win you to his position. He believes in the doctrine of Biblical infallibility, especially the verbal infallibility of the King James Version of the Bible.

Historically he has often been an opponent of science, especially any science that raised doubts about the historical and scientific accuracy of such stories as the Garden of Eden or Jonah and the whale. He has refused to accept the theory of evolution, and has sometimes been an opponent of education itself. Some fundamentalists discourage young ministers from going on for higher education on the grounds that the more education they get the more religion they lose.

Fundamentalists are the ones who have given the church the reputation of being stuffy. They are inclined to say that a good Christian is to be identified by the fact that he doesn't smoke, swear, dance, or play cards.

Many people have been imprisoned in fundamentalism. Its rigid restrictions have not released them for a life of joy and fulfillment, but confined and limited them. That's why so many have run from it. It is like escaping from prison. Usually when someone says he has broken away from the church, or given up religion, he means he has broken out of a fundamentalist strait-jacket, and not realizing there was any other approach to religion, has left the church altogether.

Some fundamentalists are generous in their attitudes, and easy to live with. My own parents would be classified as fundamentalists, I suppose. But while they tried to bring up their children to hold the same beliefs, they did not force their convictions on us or on people outside the family.

However, in my experience, the most rigid fundamentalists have a temperamental likeness to two other groups: Communists and extreme right-wingers. I have been called on by representatives of all three, and while they may be violently opposed to each other, they have all been alike in these particulars:

1. All of them are dogmatic. They are dead-sure they are right and are not interested in *discussing a question* but in *propagandizing a dogma.*

2. All of them are authoritative. They quote some authority which they consider to be unimpeachable, and accept the ideas of this authority no matter how unreasonable or how much opposing evidence is brought to their attention.

3. All of them are bold in their efforts to put you on the spot, to get you either to affirm their position so they can claim you, or to affirm an opposing position so they can discredit you.

4. All of them are short on a sense of humor. They can't take a joke. I have tried in personal contacts with all three to relieve the dead-in-earnest, demanding attitude with which they approach me by smiling warmly or turning a bit of the conversation to its humorous side. But there was no answering smile, no evidence of understanding or appreciating humor, without which life can never be put into proper perspective. And, as a character in a recent novel puts it, "I'm frightened of people who don't laugh."

Nevertheless, fundamentalism has its virtues. It puts a healthy stress on the importance of Bible study. It emphasizes the importance of prayer and a personal relationship to God. It insists on a decision, and has little patience with religious lukewarmness. It accepts no halfhearted Christians, but asks a man to make a full commitment of himself to Christ. And it has a healthy passion for winning souls. That is a constructive endeavor to which the rest of us might address more of our attention.

The second current theological emphasis is *liberalism.* If the fundamentalist is the man with the open Bible, the liberal is the man with the open mind. He wants to find the truth, and he is willing to look for it anywhere. His principal problem is that he is so afraid he might embrace a false idea that he hesitates to settle on anything as final, lest he be caught with a conviction that would subsequently be found to be false.

But at its best, liberalism takes a strong stand on positive values. It demands honest-mindedness and scorns all forms of self-deception and rationalization. It seeks to be fair, not only to all persons, but to all points of view. It believes in reason, and is unwilling to embrace a faith that demands the acceptance of ideas that are irrational.

The liberal is an apostle of the scientific method of discovering truth, and he applies it to the study of religion. He doesn't accept the Bible at face value, or quote the Bible to prove the Bible. He wants to know who wrote its various books, and when, and under what conditions. He wants to make sure that his translations are accurate and that he has the benefit of the best scholarship. He doesn't learn his science from the Bible or expect Bible writers to be authorities on the shape of the earth. He learns from his geology and biology textbooks *how* God created the world; he learns from his Bible *that* he did it. He learns from his psychology books about the subconscious within him; he learns from the Bible about the Kingdom of God within him. He learns from space science about the vastness of the universe; he learns from the Bible about the greatness of God. For him, science and religion are not in conflict. They complement one another.

The liberals have been the great proponents of the brotherhood of man, the application of religion to society as well as to the individual, the unity of the churches, and the application of reason to matters of religion.

A third theological trend is *neo-orthodoxy*. If liberalism is a reaction to fundamentalism, neo-orthodoxy is a reaction to liberalism. It is not a swing back to fundamentalism, but a move toward a restatement of the Christian religion with more definiteness than the liberal gives it, but less credulity than is characteristic of the fundamentalist.

The neo-orthodox theologian begins with faith rather than reason. He believes that reason is useful within a limited sphere, but that the most important truths come by way of revelation. Consequently, he mistrusts all philosophical systems as inadequate methods for discovering truth.

Neo-orthodoxy puts great emphasis on the gulf that exists between man and God, and even between God and the world. It refers to God as "wholly other," and maintains he is so utterly different from us that there is no possibility of man crossing the chasm and finding God. However, God can cross the chasm, and did so in Jesus Christ. But the initiative is always in God's hands, never in man's.

Great stress is also placed on man's sin. Some of the neo-orthodox theologians go so far as to say that everything a man does is a sin. Pride in particular is pointed out as the greatest sin of all because it is interpreted as man's attempt to play God.

Man, according to the neo-orthodox view, is quite helpless. He cannot by his own efforts achieve anything. He certainly can't "build the Kingdom of God." If the Kingdom of God is to come, it will be God's intervention that brings it, not man's works. Yet the devotees of neo-orthodoxy are strong on social action. This is a mystery, for there is no logic in working for social betterment if man can't do anything about it anyway. But logical consistency is the least of the worries of neo-orthodox theologians since God is beyond human reason.

This theological position may sound strange to you. But it is the point of view of some of the world's brilliant theologians, and all of us must acknowledge our indebtedness to it. It has awakened the liberal from his casual attitude about the Bible, and stimulated a profounder study of it. It has caused the church to modify its superficial attitude about the love of God, and driven it to a sharp awareness of man's sin and God's judgment. It has enlivened the field of theology, causing secular thinkers to listen more attentively than they did to the liberals. And it has reminded us all of our utter dependence upon God.

Nevertheless, for many of us, neo-orthodoxy is too vague, too negative, and, strangely, in view of its emphasis on the sin of pride, too arrogant! It has been a needed corrective to a superficial liberalism, but I am glad its day of dominance is passing.

That brings us to a more recent theological enthusiasm: *existentialism*. This, too, is a difficult term to define. Perhaps it is best to say that it comes from the word "existence" and begins with the reality of one's own being. Another way to say it is that it means involvement. The existentialist is not content to view life objectively only, as the scientist, or even the philosopher might, but subjectively. His belief is that you cannot know life except as you experience it. You must know it from the inside.

Existentialism reaches beyond theology and expresses itself in other intellectual disciplines such as literature and art. It has much to teach us. It points toward a feeling experience of truth as well as an intellectual grasp of it. But like the other theological trends it is limited in what it has to offer, and will pass.

Currently there is much talk about *Biblical theology*. This is not so much another in a succession of theological emphases as a synthesis of them. It has grown in part out of the ecumenical movement and the attempt of the various branches of Christendom to find a meeting ground in the roots of the faith of all of us.

The emphasis on Biblical theology has had the effect of correcting two previous errors. One was the mistake of the fundamentalists in taking the Scripture too literally and thereby losing its message. The other was the mistake growing out of liberalism's scientific and historical examination of the Bible with its easy dismissal of the divine implications in it. Biblical theology joins the liberal in extensive scientific study *about* the Bible, and the fundamentalist in a confident faith *in* the Bible. It puts its emphasis, not on isolated details or out-of-context segments of the Scripture, but on the total message of it.

We must, therefore, study all of the theological trends

that are prominent today. Each is the successor to another in that they seem to rise to the ascendancy one at a time. And yet they exist concurrently, sometimes battling with each other, and sometimes merging into one great river of thought and faith. They might be seen as a team of horses drawing a wagon. Each horse is spirited, and tempted to try to pull the whole load by itself, yet the wagon moves forward best when they pull together, each drawing his share of the weight.

Someone may wish that there were only one true theology that everyone could follow. It's a futile wish. Such unity will never be. Besides, our different schools of thought are not a testimony to our weakness but to God's magnificence. He is too great to be comprehended by any one system of thought. No sooner is one theology created than another sees its weaknesses and enters the field as a corrective. Truth is many-sided, and we have to approach it from different angles. The rising and falling of different theologies is a healthy thing, as is the coexistence of competing theologies.

So choose your own theology: fundamentalism, liberalism, neo-orthodoxy, existentialism, a combination of these, or something quite different from any of them. But remember the counsel of Robert Frost when he said, "Don't be an agnostic. Be *something!*"

Laymen need to accept this challenge because the temptation is for them to avoid such definite commitment. While they have been exposed to theological ideas in sermons and Sunday-school lessons all of their lives, any serious and systematic study of theology by laymen generally is something new in most denominations. But it is an important part of that growing force that is revolutionizing the church. Laymen are studying theology with a new seriousness. Many of them bring to this study a background of academic and professional achievement in other fields, giving them an advantage that few clergymen have had.

Being a grass-roots sort of thing, this new enthusiasm of laymen for theology is expressed in many different ways.

We are in the creative period of the movement, which is the most exciting time for anything. Some laymen approach it vocationally, gathering together in homogeneous groups of doctors or lawyers or teachers. Lay schools of theology are being established by some of the theological seminaries where the schools' top professors offer laymen the same courses required of ministerial students. Small groups within local churches meet regularly for study of the Bible and some of the best books on theology. Some of the established Sunday-school classes in the adult division of local church schools have geared their programs to this kind of intensive study. Most people interested in the new movement, however, have found it easier to start new groups than to change the approach of the old ones.

However he may approach it, the church member who is serious about being the best layman he can be will take advantage of this new emphasis on the study of theology among the laymen and accept the challenge to become oriented theologically. Until he does, he is more of a burden to the church than a help to it. Hard work in the church is not enough. One must work hard at the right thing for the right reasons to achieve the right goal.

Special attention given to theology will help to accomplish this, but it is important to remember that no theology encompasses final truth. The best that can be hoped for is that it points toward it. Theological enthusiasms come and go, but the God whom we serve remains constant. In the last analysis, it is not to one theology as over against another that we are called to be loyal, but to the God of Jesus Christ whom all theologies seek to understand and no theology fully explains. Theology leads toward God only when it remains open-ended. It is a worthy servant of God only when it directs its students beyond the classroom to Christ-like actions. When we say that theology is central, we mean that the God of Jesus Christ is central, and theology at its best leads us to Him.

IV

The Sunday Service Is Central

If our purpose is to remain clear, and if it is to be the measuring stick for all we do, we must find ways of keeping it vividly before us. Christians have always found corporate worship the best means of accomplishing this. That is why, in Protestant Christianity, Sunday worship in the sanctuary is central. It is for worship, more than any other one thing, that the church gathers its members together. By worship we mean acknowledging the sovereignty of God, seeking to know the will of God, and offering ourselves to God.

Around this center is the great educational and service program, strengthening, supporting, and expressing, but never replacing the central function of the church. Church-school classes and program activities might be compared with the flying buttresses on a Gothic cathedral. They support and strengthen the sanctuary and even express some of its essential beauty. The structure would collapse without them. But they are not the sanctuary, and to treat them as such—to care for, enhance, and strengthen the buttresses—while letting the sanctuary fall into ruin is to emerge with a monstrosity. It would be an accumulation of strong supports that no longer hold anything up.

The first commitment of every sincere church member is to attend Sunday services regularly. Every teacher and worker in the church school should teach by example that no Christian's week is complete without participation in the great act of corporate worship. Every organization within the local church should remind its members repeatedly that their first obligation to this smaller group of which they are a part is to take their place in the sanctuary of the church at the hour of worship each Sunday morning. Every youth should put church attendance "first" on his weekly calendar, and every child should learn from the time he is quite young the thrill of corporate worship.

Most Protestants take church attendance too lightly. "I never go to church now because I was forced to when I was young" is an excuse we have all heard, but it has little validity. At best it is an oversimplification. At worst it represents a total misreading of the facts. Many people stay away from church because they were not taken often enough as children to develop a taste for it. Few stay away because they were given an overdose.

Nevertheless, the superstition persists that too much church in childhood hardens the adult forever against active participation in any form of organized religion. This is unfortunate, not simply because the individual's clinging to the superstition is impoverishing himself, but even more because he frightens young parents into keeping their own children away from church services.

I like to see children in church. I am not referring to infants, of course. Most churches today maintain excellent nurseries for the care of preschool children during the church worship hour, and parents should take advantage of this service. But as soon as they are old enough to sense the reverence and importance of a service of worship children should begin to participate in it. They won't understand everything that is said or done in the sanctuary, I know, but then, their parents and grandparents may not understand it all either. Great religion always has an element of wonder and of mystery about it. From the time they are very young children can develop a feeling for the hallowed experience of public worship. They can learn to know and love the great hymns and to appreciate fine organ and choral music. They can see their parents with bowed heads and develop a feeling for the sacredness of holy scripture. Even the sermon, which is most frequently singled out as uninteresting to them, normally contains portions which catch their attention and develop their religious insight.

In our family we have followed the policy of bringing the children to church services from the time they entered the first grade. For the first few years they wiggled a bit, and my wife admits that this sometimes interfered with her own worship. But they were never a real disturbance, and to keep them from distracting others even a little, she used to sit with them in the balcony until they were old enough to move with her to a position nearer the pulpit where she prefers to sit. When she sensed that they were getting a little restless, she often handed them a pencil and paper so they could draw a few pictures to siphon off their excess energy. But this did not mean they were paying no attention to the worship. From the beginning they came home with comments and questions that indicated real involvement.

So I like for parents to bring their children to church and, while not confining them to any strait-jacket, expect them to remain respectfully quiet throughout the worship hour. Does that sound old-fashioned? Actually it can't possibly be either old-fashioned or new-fashioned because it isn't a matter of fashion at all. It is a matter of religion. Not only in the church school, but also in the Sunday morning services of worship, we should "train up a child in the way he should go" (Prov. 22:6), and if we can depend on the scripture, "when he is old he will not depart from it" (Prov. 22:6).

A generation raised on the half-truth that compulsion is bad finds it difficult to understand that to do the right thing through a sense of duty is better than not to do it at all. It would be ideal, I suppose, if every church member attended church every Sunday simply because he would rather do that than anything else he could think of. For that matter, it would be nice if children went to school and did the dishes only because they wanted to, and if adults always went to work, paid their bills, and remained true to their spouses because they never had the slightest desire to do anything else. But life isn't put together that way. A man of character does the right thing because it is right, not because it is more pleasant than any alternative he can think of. If it is right and pleasant too, he is fortunate. But pleasant or not, if it is the right thing to do, he does it. This is not to infer that it is more fun to sin than to be good. On the contrary, the gospel is "good news of a great joy" (Luke 2:10), but the joy of goodness is sometimes less apparent or at least less immediate than the "pleasures" of evil-doing.

This applies to Sunday worship the same as to anything else of true value. Once, after he had completed a series of sermons on worship, Raymond Abba was approached by a young man who asked, "Do you think I ought to come to church when I don't feel like it? There are times when I want to come and really enjoy the service, but there are other times when I've no inclination at all. Wouldn't it be hypocritical to come then?" Dr. Abba replied, "Well John, do you only pay the grocer's bill and the rent when you feel like it?" Later he observed, "Worship is a debt to be discharged independently of our feelings; it is giving unto the Lord the glory DUE unto His name; hence 'it is obligatory on Christians.' The primary purpose of worship is the glory of God, not the edification of man; 'God must come first, or man's edification will not follow.' "[1]

Nevertheless, whether obligatory or voluntary, to enter the sanctuary for worship should be the high moment in every Protestant layman's week. It should be the high-water mark to which he refers in retrospect when the demands of his daily routine deplete his spiritual resources, the summit to which he lifts his eyes in hourly anticipation. It should be for him what Isaiah must have expected it to be when he declared, "Thus says the Lord: '. . . my house shall be called a house of prayer for all peoples' " (Isa. 56:7). In those simple words the prophet established forever the true nature of a house of worship. It is a place for God and man to meet. It is a place to pray.

Unfortunately, however, people sometimes forget that. By the time Jesus came into the picture, they had forgotten; so he reminded them. Driving the merchants and money-changers from the temple, he quoted the words of Isaiah which they probably knew but disregarded: "My house shall be called a house of prayer . . ." (Isa. 56:7), then added his own accusation, "but you make it a den of robbers" (Matt. 21:13).

Who were these people who had desecrated the house of worship? And in what way were they robbers? I'll tell you who I think they were. In all probability they were religious folks, faithful adherents to the faith they were destroying, but they were robbing sincere worshipers of their chance to commune in peace with God. There is no reason to believe there was any graft involved in what they were doing. Their activities may even have been organized by the church administrator. In any event, they were working in close cooperation with the temple leaders. And they were rendering a service. A part of Jewish worship was the presentation of suitably cleansed animals as a sacrifice. By making these

[1] *Principles of Christian Worship* (London: Oxford University Press, 1957), p. 12.

available at the temple door, they spared worshipers the inconvenience of bringing them through the crowded streets of Jerusalem. Similarly, the old Hebrew coins, required for use in the temple, were different from the money in general circulation, so you can see at once how convenient it was for the worshiper to step up to the money-changer's table right there in the temple court and exchange what was in his pocket for what would be acceptable in the temple. There is little reason to believe that what the merchants and money-changers were doing was so bad in itself. It was bad because it was interfering with worship.

It is easy to see how it happened because something similar has taken place in our day. Gradually, almost imperceptibly, without anyone's meaning any offense by it, elements not congenial to worship have slipped into the worship hour. A special announcement here, a promotional stunt there, a bit of friendly conversation in the pews, and someone's worship has been interrupted. To the extent that we introduce these distractions into the worship hour we are thieves in the temple, robbing the worshipers of their chance to worship as they ought. These intrusions have become so common in Protestant worship that some people think they belong there. As a consequence, we have developed a generation of Christians who scarcely know how to worship at all.

Most of them attend a worship service as they attend a movie—as spectators rather than participants. They come to be entertained, and depart to pass judgment on the artistry of the performers. They do not come to church to worship. They come to witness a program with a religious theme. They are not, in the true sense, worshipers. They are churchgoers. For them, if a service is more pleasing than irritating, it is a successful worship experience.

The problem is that they use secular standards to judge a spiritual experience. The minister is judged as a speaker, the organist as a musician, and the service as a performance. The true worshiper, on the other hand, while he appreciates artistry, never judges a service of worship by its leaders but by his own encounter with God. It is possible for a service to be perfectly put together by all secular standards of music, speech, and interior decoration, and lead the worshiper not one step nearer God. And it is possible for a worshiper to hear a sermon that is clumsily put together and music that is out of balance and be conscious only of the fact that he is a part of a worshiping congregation to whom God is speaking.

Do not misunderstand me. I am something of a perfectionist about worship services myself. I believe no minister has a right to step into the pulpit unless he is well prepared and can communicate the gospel with some conviction and power. I believe church music should be as fine as can be heard anywhere. I am convinced that the artistry of flower arrangement and efficiency of ushering can be a glorious ministry. I covet for my church the best in worship. But the purpose of all of this is not to draw attention to the leaders of worship but to focus the mind of the worshiper on God and open the heart of the worshiper to hear the word of God. Failing in this, the finest speakers and musicians are nothing but performers. Succeeding in it, even the poorest ones belong in the company of saints.

One time Leslie Weatherhead, while talking with a young man who was studying for the ministry, asked him what had led him into that calling. The young man replied that it was a sermon he had heard at Kingswood School when he was a boy. "Who was the preacher?" asked Weatherhead, who comments, "I can remember now his clear eyes, as he looked at me and said, 'I can't remember.' I was astonished at his answer and still find it hard to believe that the words were spoken, but they were spoken and they were quite sincere. 'I only know that God spoke to me that night,' he said simply."[2] That's the way it should be. Leaders of worship should be of the highest quality, and

[2] *City Temple Tidings,* Sept. 9, 1951.

worthy of commendation, but they should inspire the worshipers to leave a service singing not their praises, but God's.

Modern man needs worship experiences like that. Beneath his façade of smart dress and sharp wit his soul stands and trembles. Behind his friendly smile and his grand act of generosity, his real self waits and wonders about God. Jerked and jostled by competing demands, confused by contradictory voices, beaten down by disappointment, buried in fear, the immortal soul of modern man crouches in its corner and looks for God.

It is the function of worship to take man by the hand, and lead him past his fears, his habits, his disappointments, his confusions, his feelings of inferiority, until he stands in the throne room of the eternal God. There at last God's finger can probe the soul and ferret out its tender spots. There man can find meaning in his existence, purpose for his endeavor, and strength to walk the long hard road. That's what should happen in a house of prayer. But how can we make it happen?

That's a job for each layman to assume for himself. If he is to have this experience he must take the initiative.

For one thing, he must learn to enter the sanctuary in a mood of quiet expectancy. That may be a good deal to expect from most Protestants, but they can do it.

It is said that the founder of the Cistercian Order always stood a few moments in silence by the sanctuary door before he opened it. No one knew exactly what was in his mind in those moments, but it was assumed he was preparing himself for the greatness of the thing that would happen to him on the other side of the door. Soon his monks took up the habit, until it became an established practice among them to pause outside the sanctuary door, silence their minds and spirits, and then enter into the presence of the Lord God Almighty.

The Jews traditionally prepare themselves the night before so that in quiet slumber the spirit of God may move in their hearts and as the Sabbath dawns they will be ready to enter the synagogue. Roman Catholics commonly enter their church in silence, kneel, and cross themselves as individually they acknowledge the majesty of God. But many Protestants continue to rush into the sanctuary, chatting all the way, and with less of a sense that this is something special than when an attractive hostess ushers them to their seats in a nice restaurant. Certainly they have a less clearly defined notion of why they are there than when they enter the marble-floored, dome-ceilinged bank on Monday morning.

Not many of us would enter a home with dirty shoes, but we often enter the sanctuary with the petty accumulations of a week clinging to our spirits. As a kind of divine courtesy, we should linger at the door long enough to clean them off. We should shake ourselves free of our social calendars, our business files, our work schedules, our animosities, and our infatuations that so regularly clutter our minds, and prepare to see God only. Someone has suggested that this may be what is meant by entering the closet and shutting the door. When we walk into the sanctuary of the church, we are closeted with God. We should shut the door against the distractions of daily life.

No one should enter the sanctuary of the church as he would enter a social hall, expecting to visit. He should not come to church as he would go to an opera house for quality entertainment. He should not approach worship as he would go to the office with a mental list of things to do. He should enter as a worshiper, prepared to humble himself before the Almighty.

A second thing the layman must do if he is to find worship a meaningful experience is to assume responsibility for the effectiveness of his own worship.

Drawing an analogy from the theater, Søren Kierkegaard points out that as the actor strides prominently onto the stage, drawing every eye to himself, there is another in the wings waiting to prompt him. He is the inconspicuous one, wishing to be overlooked. The actor is the one proclaiming the message, but when he hesitates, or forgets, words are put in his mouth "by the hidden one that sits and whispers."

Now it is common for laymen to look upon the preacher as the actor and to see themselves as theatergoers who are on hand for the performance. But, says Kierkegaard, this is all wrong. "The speaker is not the actor—not in the remotest sense. No, the speaker is the prompter." In a service of worship, the worshipers are on the stage and their audience is God. The minister's role is only that of the prompter, whispering from the sidelines: "Praise God—Confess your sins—Ask Him for help—Dedicate yourself." But the praising, the confessing, the asking and the dedicating are the acts of the worshipers.

So many people think of a worship service as a passive experience. After all, they sit through most of it. They listen to a sermon someone else has prepared and delivered; they enjoy music others have rehearsed. To be sure, they join in an occasional hymn or the reading of a unison prayer or affirmation of faith, but their voices are lost among the others. All in all, little effort is required of them. They don't even have to find a seat for themselves, or take their own offering to the altar. These services are all provided for them.

This concept is all wrong. True worship is an aggressive act. It is hard work to listen intelligently to a sermon, place its precepts against one's own life, and, if necessary, change one's customary patterns of thinking to come closer to the Christian ideal. It is hard to catch the hidden secrets in the scripture that is read, to pray meaningfully during periods of silence, and to imbue the Lord's Prayer with fresh life and meaning each time it is repeated. It is a life-shaking experience each time one peels the protective covering from his soul, exposing it to God. It is hard, but it is worship. The only time worship is easy for people is when they aren't worshiping. If they put no strain into it, they get no inspiration out of it. God's house is a house of prayer, and contrary to those who think that prayer is nothing more than an inexpensive tranquilizer, we are followers of one who, at least on one occasion, prayed with such intensity that his sweat fell from him like drops of blood. He was involved in an aggressive act, a personal encounter with God.

A third thing the layman must do if he is to worship meaningfully is to accept the worshiping fellowship. To be sure there is a place for prayer when one is completely alone, but this is no substitute for worship that is shared with others.

A very important part of a church service is the person sitting beside us. He is there, at least in part, to lead us closer to God. Every person in the room can add to the significance of our worship experience. Each has something to say to us. Those we love are saying, "We enter God's presence together, and our love is strengthened." Our enemy is saying, "You can only approach the throne of God if you take me with you." The person whose skin is a different color from our own is reminding us that all races are God's children. As the congregation sings and prays together, we are reminded that we praise God best when we do it in fellowship.

The presence of others keeps us alert to their needs. There is a folk song from Africa that our young people like to sing. It is called "Kum Ba Yah" and begins, "Kum ba yah, my Lord, kum ba yah," which means "Come by here, my Lord, come by here." This should be the prayer of every layman throughout a worship service. As the folk song moves from verse to verse, it describes the many human situations in which people find themselves, always concluding with a call for God's presence with them: "Someone's crying Lord, kum ba yah." "Someone's praying Lord, kum ba yah." "Someone's singing Lord, kum ba yah."

Any layman who uses the basic thought of this simple folk song as he sits in church each Sunday will find it opening the door to glorious experience. He will begin to notice the people around him—not in the way he noticed them before, to comment on the way they looked or acted—but with eyes that see the soul. Where he sees sadness he'll sing, though none can hear him, "Someone's crying Lord, kum ba yah." And where he perceives that for others the service of worship is a celebration of some high joy, he'll pray, "Someone's singing Lord, kum ba yah." Thus with tentacles of prayer he will embrace a congregation, lifting them toward God. And strangely, they will have lifted him as well.

That's what happened in Berlin not long ago. There is a church there whose property was bisected by the Berlin wall, leaving the church in East Berlin and the parsonage in West Berlin. As Reformation Day approached, the church youth of the Western sector decided to gather at the parsonage and form a choir to sing the hymn of the Reformation, Luther's "A Mighty Fortress Is Our God." It was their hope that their Christian brothers, meeting in the church on the other side of the wall, would hear their singing and know they were standing by. But somehow, word of their plan had seeped through the wall to the Christian youth of the Eastern sector, so they too assembled as large a crowd as they could get together. And just before the Western choir were ready to sing "A Mighty Fortress," the Eastern choir began to sing an old Reformation hymn that had not been sung in churches for a century or more but which had recently been recovered because it spoke to the need of the German church today. This is what they sang:

> I can't go on.
> No comfort here abideth,
> Life's burden weighs me down
> It is too much!
> I cannot find relief
> All comfort takes its leave!
> Have mercy on me, Lord!
> I can't go on!

Quickly the Western choir changed their plan and picked up the second stanza of the hymn and sang it in answer to the cry of the youth in the East:

> You can go on!
> God's help will soon be there.
> He'll turn you from your grief
> And give you peace.
> You just must keep on fighting.
> Our Lord too suffered in His stride.
> Go on with Him—He's on your side.
> You can go on!

Again the Easterners picked up the tune with the third stanza and its repeated cry, "I can't go on," and then they joined with the Westerners as all sang together, though separated by a wall of stone, chipped glass, and barbed wire,

> You can go on!
> There soon will be an end.
> God reaches out His hand,
> Look here—His hand, to you!
> Ah, let us pray and pray.
> And He will send the day.
> His help will make us say,
> To Him be praise,
> He is our strength and stay.

We too must "pray and pray and pray," for whatever our lot, we can find strength in the shared prayers of the worshiping fellowship. Let no layman forget the words of Isaiah, repeated again by our Lord: "My house shall be called a house of prayer for all peoples" (Isa. 56:7).

Now a word of caution. Worship may be the most wonderful experience a layman can have, but it can also fall short of his expectations. He must learn to accept its glories with humble thanks, and its disappointments with faith. Not every church service he attends will be his Damascus Road, his Aldersgate, but any one might be. It is very easy for a Christian, as he reaches up toward God, to expect too much. At least he sometimes expects something other than what is available. I recall a man in the church of my childhood who was always troubled because he hadn't had an experience like that of St. Paul. He was asking for too much. God speaks to each person in an individual way and in his own good time. It is better to be faithful in fulfilling one's religious duty but modest in what one expects. The hymn has the right idea:

> I ask no dream
>   no prophet ecstasy,
> No sudden rending
>   of the veil of clay
> No angel visitant,
>   no opening skies,
> But take the dimness
>   of my soul away.

John Wesley had a good deal to say about the patience necessary for anyone seeking spiritual fulfillment. The longer he lived, the less dogmatic he became about the rewards that would come to the faithful in this life. Dr. K. Morgan Edwards has called attention to his changing attitude. He says:

> When he first wrote on Christian perfection, Wesley thought that the mature Christian would never ask for relief from pain. In the later edition he added a footnote: "This is too strong. Our Lord himself desired ease in pain."
>
> Wesley once believed that the mature Christian's thought would not wander during prayer. In the edi-

tion of 1777 he wrote a footnote: "This is far too strong," and called attention to one of his later sermons entitled, "Wandering Thoughts."

Before Aldersgate, Wesley believed that the mature Christian would not be perplexed about what he was to do. The Holy Spirit would tell him hourly what to do and say. In the last edition he added the sad footnote, ". . . not always."

Thirteen years before Aldersgate, Wesley felt that after a man has made the great surrender, he would never be tempted again. Forty years after Aldersgate, Wesley admitted that sometimes we are tempted "grievously."[3]

Similarly, a devoted missionary in South America wrote in his diary, "We are well settled by now. Life gets to be a routine of buying, selling, treating sick, fixing kerosene and gasoline appliances, trying to learn a language. It's a fight to try to get time for the latter. Also time for Bible study and prayer. It's hard to stay on top of it all, hard to keep rejoicing, hard to love these ungrateful Indians. It's hard to keep our primary purpose in view when we get so swamped with secondary things."

That's the cry of every layman. It *is* hard to keep our primary purpose in view when we get so swamped with secondary things. But the church's service of worship can help to accomplish that purpose.

It has done so for a friend of mine. She writes:

For me, regular attendance at the Sunday morning worship service has contributed more than its proportionate share to whatever spiritual development I've experienced. It has assured me of at least 52 hours a year given over to thoughts of God and His will for my life.

[3] *Hoping to Be Somebody* (Nashville: Abingdon Press, 1959), pp. 98 f.

There are several ways in which I try to get the most from this hour on Sunday. First, I go believing that God has a word for me that day, and I listen for it in the hymns, in the special music, in the Scripture and prayers, and in the sermon. Secondly, I pray for the minister and the choir, that they may be keenly aware that they are channels through which God can reach the people who are gathered there. And then I always pray for "us," the congregation, that our spirits may be alert and our hearts open for the Truth. There has been no spectacular, instantaneous spiritual experience for me as a result of my many years of regular attendance at church. Rather, there has been a steady building up of spiritual reserves which have sustained me in times of adversity and prosperity, in periods of joy and sorrow, and in moments of strength and weakness.

That is a testimony with simple eloquence, as is also the answer the deaf-mute gave to the question, "Why do you come to church each Sunday when you cannot hear the service?" He wrote his answer: "I come each week to let people know which side I am on."

The true fellowship of the church—the genuine love of member for member and members for God—is expressed most profoundly when, in the steady rhythm of a seven-day cycle, churchmen return from their various stations of ministry in the world, the office, the home, the school, the shop, and gather together for corporate worship. They are the blood of Christ's body. Returning from "foot" and "hand" and "brain" to be purified in the sanctuary, as in lungs filled with clean air, they enter the heart, the service of worship, and with the mighty throb of it are sent forth renewed, with added power, to spend themselves in service, and then return again in joyous repetition of this age-old, life-renewing, life-sustaining cycle. Once fully engaged in, the drama of it is breathtaking. Think of a group of Christians whose various lay ministries of the past six days have included visiting a murderer in prison, risking one's life in a civil rights effort, helping a pregnant high school girl find counsel and hope, praying by a bedside where an old man fights the death he seeks, guiding a group of business associates to choose a more ethical procedure than they had planned, and witnessing for truth in a political meeting in which the shouting is on the other side. From these and several hundred more individual experiences of putting Christianity to work in daily life, these good friends gather for worship.

Silently they stand together as appropriate scripture sentences are spoken by the minister:

> Draw near to God and he will draw near to you.
> Humble yourselves before the Lord and he will exalt you. (Jas. 4:8, 10)

The organ is heard, and in a moment, memories of the week's ministries still fresh in their minds, the worshipers are singing:

> And are we yet alive
> And see each other's face?
> Glory and thanks to Jesus give,
> For his almighty grace.
>
> What troubles have we seen,
> What mighty conflicts past,
> Fightings without, and fears within,
> Since we assembled last!
>
> Yet out of all the Lord
> Hath brought us by his love;
> And still he doth his help afford,
> And hides our life above.
>
> Then let us make our boast
> Of his redeeming power,
> Which saves us to the uttermost,
> Till we can sin no more.

Let us take up the cross,
Till we the crown obtain,
And gladly reckon all things loss,
So we may Jesus gain.[4]

One worshiper looks at another who he knows has won a battle with sin that week, and smiles almost imperceptibly, with gentle reassurance. Another, remembering a dear member of the fellowship who is not "yet alive" closes his eyes as cover for a tear. And a youth, suddenly grateful for God's power to see him through each trying week in its turn, squares his shoulders with new courage and deep joy.

The congregation is seated and prayer is said. In intercession, loved ones are remembered by name, and petition is made for the worshipers themselves for strength to meet the challenge of each day.

Tithes and offerings are laid on the altar in solemn dedication; scripture is read, then meaningfully interpreted in a sermon that applies the ancient words to problems the worshipers are likely to encounter before another Sabbath takes its turn. It sets their compass on the spirit's north star, and gives them courage to believe they can sail from port again in hope of a triumphant voyage and a safe return.

Once more all voices join in singing and they approach what Paul Van Burn calls "the holiest moment in the service of worship." That is, "the moment when the Church gets up and goes out of the doors of the church building into the world." In deep awareness of purpose, the worshipers repeat,

The Spirit of the Lord is upon me, because he has anointed me to preach good news to the poor. He has sent me to proclaim release to the captives and recov-

[4] Charles Wesley. *The Methodist Hymnal* (Nashville: The Methodist Book Concern, 1964, 1966), p. 336.

ering of sight to the blind, to set at liberty those who are oppressed, to proclaim the acceptable year of the Lord. (Luke 4:18–19)

And the minister sets forth the challenge that is at once a blessing and a command:

Go forth into the world in peace;
be of good courage;
hold fast that which is good;
render to no man evil for evil;
strengthen the faint-hearted;
support the weak;
help the afflicted;
honour all men;
Love and serve the Lord,
rejoicing in the pow'r of the Holy Spirit.
And the blessing of God almighty, the Father,
the Son, and the Holy Ghost be upon you,
and remain with you for ever. Amen.[5]

In the high act of corporate worship, more than at any other time or in any other way, the fellowship of churchmen becomes the fellowship of love.

[5] Martin Shaw, "A Blessing" (an anthem published in the United States by G. Schirmer, Inc., New York, 1927; London: J. Curwen and Sons, Ltd.). Copyright 1927 by Martin Shaw. Reprinted by permission of the publishers: J. Curwen & Sons, London.

V

Lifting the Level of Preaching

As corporate worship is central in the Christian life, the sermon is central in worship. In the last analysis, conducting public worship is the minister's primary responsibility, and the preparation and delivery of the sermon is at the heart of it. The minister is a "spokesman of the Lord." There is nothing about our high-speed, technological age to change that simple fact.

Not everyone will agree with this high estimate of preaching. This is evident in the widespread use of the word as a synonym for nagging. If a parent delivers a harangue to his son on what he presumes to be his duty, the boy is likely to retort, "Quit preaching." When my son was elected Yell King in his high school, the vice-principal commented that he got his training for it from his father. That is fair enough humor, and was given and received in good grace. But it does suggest the opinion of many that preaching is yelling.

Others, including some but by no means all professors

in our theological seminaries, also take a dim view of it. They try to make teachers rather than preachers out of their best students. The others, they prepare for that vague designation of "the parish ministry" which means everything and nothing. While most of our accredited seminaries are top quality academic institutions, they are not all tooled for producing great preachers. The reason would appear to be that the religious academic community as a whole is no longer convinced of its importance. Martin E. Marty says that theological educators can meet to discuss ways of improving the ministry and "can talk for a week and not mention preaching. . . ." Sometimes it seems that those who are doing most to behead the prophet are those who should be perfecting him. When one seminary professor dealt with the subject, he said that laymen "are unlikely to hear the radical demands of the gospel in a brief and easily ignored sermon." "Brief and easily ignored" were evidently modifiers he would apply generally to modern preaching. With preaching thus simply disposed of, he confessed: "Some place must be found where the deepest needs of individuals may be met and where they may be met in terms of the gospel." He had his answer: "The small fellowship-study groups appear to be the form it is most likely to take."

I am all for "the small fellowship-study groups," but I don't consider them to be a substitute for preaching. And I have a growing conviction that preaching is not being downgraded because it is ineffective; it is becoming ineffective because it is being downgraded. Even men who occupy the pulpit Sunday after Sunday sometimes treat it as though it were of slight significance. I once saw a slogan on a minister's study wall which read, "An ounce of performance is worth a pound of preaching." That is thin inspiration for great preaching. To me it said, "I'm not much of a preacher, but I surely keep busy." If the minister has no greater respect for the pulpit than this he should not be surprised if others take his claim to preach the unsearchable riches of Christ as a bit of a joke.

Kyle Haselden[1] says that "preaching is in the doldrums" in this country just now and preachers themselves don't care. He says they preach because that's what's expected of them, and they do it well enough to get by, but they have little sense of being under God's appointment to communicate an eternal message. He concedes that it may be true, as some say, that the general level of preaching is higher now than previously, but he maintains that this only means that it "is stagnating on a high plateau." Insisting that there are no preachers in America today with the effectiveness and influence of men who preached a few years back, he says that whenever he invites people to name the great preachers of present day America, they name Fosdick, Scherer, Buttrick, and Sockman, "every one of whom was in his heyday a quarter of a century ago."

He sees the men who currently occupy the nation's pulpits as part of a generation that "is desperately searching for an adequate substitute for the sermon. . . ." Everything is tried: "film strips against a symphonic background, dial-a-prayer telephones, liturgical dances, jukeboxes in the church parlor." But he affirms, "This generation must discover for itself as others before it have that the only adequate substitute for poor preaching is good preaching."

Charles Clayton Morrison, former editor of the *Christian Century*, after making a personal survey of present-day preaching, came up with an equally gloomy description of it. Noting that ministers were more interested in counseling with one individual at a time than in saying anything significant to a respectably large gathering of Christians, he concluded: "The sermon had lost its character as an Event, either for the preacher or the congregation. It had become hardly more than a space-filling homily in a highly liturgical or folksy impromptu exercise preparatory to the coffee break."

In similar sadness, Ian Macpherson, a British clergyman,

[1] *The Urgency of Preaching* (New York: Harper & Row, 1963), pp. 17 ff.

says that preaching "is being set on one side in favor of the drapery and carpentry of a theatrical religious externalism," and expresses his regret that so many modern preachers are like the minister W. R. Maltby described. He said, "He spoke of great things and made them small, of holy things and made them common, of God and made Him of no account." And Raymond Abba writes mournfully of the sermons he hears these days. "Like rivers that wander through the desert and finally get lost in the sand," he says, "they lead nowhere."

All this is a bad sign. With some saying that today's preaching is inferior and others shrugging off all preaching as unimportant, we have a long way to go to lift this time-honored function of the clergy back to its proper position. And it is important to lift it back because, historically, the church has been no stronger than its pulpit. Its greatest days are marked by its greatest preaching.

The testimony to this truth is impressive. Paul Scherer says, "The most creative and critical ages of the church's history—the ages of Paul and the apostles, of Ambrose and Augustine, of Urban, of Luther and Calvin and Wesley and Brooks—all of these have been the great ages of Christian preaching." With similar conviction, Carl Patton, a great preacher and former professor of homiletics at the Pacific School of Religion, once declared that the leaders of the church who have really influenced human life and history "have done it by their preaching." He says that people need things to think about, ideals and convictions with power to stir the mind and enlarge the soul and that preaching is the church's way of setting those forces in motion. They "proceed out of the mouth of the Lord via the mouth of the preacher," he says, and declares that "the real output of a church is the ideas that come from its pulpit." Charles R. Brown, former Dean of Divinity School, Yale, had much the same conviction. Reviewing the history of the church, he highlighted its great achievements in architecture, liturgy, art and music, but concluded that whenever "there was lacking in all this the *living* voice of a *living* man speaking in the name and under the power of the *living* God, there came a steady irresistible decline in the religious life of that land." Let no one underestimate the crucial significance of preaching in history. Jeremiah has been given credit for bringing a new morality to an entire nation through his preaching. The preaching of Amos opened the door for new and higher standards of social justice. Paul's and Peter's preaching stimulated forces strong enough to topple empires, and subsequent social transformation with world-wide ramifications has been traced at least in part to the preaching of men like St. Francis, St. Augustine, Martin Luther, and John Wesley. In our own day, only the blind could fail to see that when Martin Luther King, armed with Biblical truth and prophetic eloquence, stands up to preach, the whole world looks and listens and is changed.

This brings us to an obvious question. If preaching was so important and effective in the past, and even today is seen to have great power in certain situations, why are most present-day ministers so absorbed with other things and so poorly prepared to preach?

Strangely enough, the answer is that they are poorly prepared for it because the church has been so successful. As it has grown in numbers, the minister has been forced to spend more time with membership records and less time on his sermons. As it has expanded its buildings and increased its budget, the minister has been called upon to give more time to architecture and finances and less time to shaping up his message for Sunday morning. As it has expanded its interests to include Christian education, counseling, and community service, it has fallen to the minister to direct these activities at the expense of his preparation for preaching. As the denominations have grown and become more complex, the local pastor is called on by headquarters to direct the work of special committees, to submit reports concerning his own congregation, and to represent denominational programs in his local parish. With each added job he has less time to prepare for his work in the pulpit. How different this is from the position of priority given to preaching a generation or two ago. Ian Macpherson reports that "when Alexander Whyte began his ministry in Glasgow, the Kirk session told him bluntly that, if faced with the alternatives of answering a summons to visit the dying or preparing his Sunday sermon, and if he could do the one or the other but not both, he ought to prepare his Sunday sermon." The laymen of that church had no question about the importance of preaching or the time it takes to prepare for it.

Things are different now; as the church has grown strong, preaching has grown weak. But the pulpit is at the heart of the church and a weakened heart cannot continue to sustain an overgrown body. It cannot even continue to beat. So we begin to hear about preachers breaking down, or leaving the pastoral ministry for some other type of work. Shortly thereafter we hear the ominous diagnosis that the church as an institution is beyond hope of renewal. All kinds of symptoms are noted: our overorganization, our attachment to the status quo, our tendency to be irrelevant to what is going on in the world, our race prejudice and our shallow theology. Almost nobody has observed that our problem is heart trouble. When we recover the power that pulsates from the pulpit, no one will worry much about a sick church.

We have a long way to go before we recover it. Some time ago I visited a large Protestant church and heard the senior minister preach. Tall and handsome, he was a commanding figure in the pulpit. He had a fine voice and was obviously sincere. But his sermon missed the mark. It wasn't bad. It wasn't good. It was organized but it wasn't well organized. It was intelligent but it wasn't moving. Based clearly on scripture, it was relevant to our time, yet it could not be defined as inspired utterance. It had no power. I am confident no one left the service that day feeling he had been struck with the fist of a righteous God or lifted in the hand of a loving Father.

What was wrong? That church had several ministers,

each with his designated responsibilties. This one was at the top of the heap and his first assignment was preaching. Yet it was obvious to me he had not done his homework. At no time did preacher and sermon merge as one. The minister was fulfilling a weekly assignment, meeting a Sunday deadline. He was not preaching. I am sure his sermon had been put together in a hurry when he was tired. I recognized the signs. It was incidental to everything else that was going on in his busy church. All the makings of a great preacher were there, but the great preacher wasn't. He had the personal magnetism, Christian dedication, speaking ability, and intelligence that are necessary, but neither he nor his laymen believed sufficiently in preaching to see that it had first place in his life, not only on Sunday, but every day of the week.

Bishop Gerald Kennedy shares my concern about the tendency of so many men to make preaching a secondary thing. Recently he sent a pastoral letter to the ministers of his area, challenging them to work harder on preaching. He said:

> The older I grow, the more I find myself running scared so far as next Sunday's sermon is concerned. Some of the brethren may find peace of mind in their preparation but I do not. Are we working with our material and making its presentation effective? So much of our stuff seems to be loose, unbuttoned and ineffective. The only answer I know is hard work and this may demand less time on some other projects. But I believe that at the end of the day we are going to win or lose according to what happens in our worship services on Sunday morning.

Now we come to the paradox of it all. While preaching is commonly downgraded and most ministers give sermon preparation a low priority in the week's scheduling, effectiveness in preaching continues to be the first requirement on the list of virtually every pulpit committee in the land. The initial question they ask about every prospect for their pulpit is, "Can he preach?" This is not surprising when you remember that one Gallup poll revealed the fact that 97 per cent of the people in this country consider the sermon to be the most important element in corporate worship.

Let no one underestimate the power of preaching. When one dedicates himself to this one task, disciplines his energies to focus upon it, and puts his life in God's hands, miracles are performed. His sermons never come up to his own hopes. He often goes into the pulpit wishing he had another day, another hour to perfect the message he is about to deliver, and when he leaves, often feels that he failed. As the years pass, however, his ministry is enriched with the memories of those whose lives were changed because he preached. Some changes are sudden and dramatic: a man planning suicide turns his eyes away from death and back to life again. Sometimes the transformation is more gradual: the narrow-minded broaden their horizons; the drifting find new purpose for their lives; the prejudiced make love their aim. The selfish learn to share. The fearful walk with greater courage. Those who are bewildered find a faith. The sorrowing find comfort, the wavering, courage and the depressed find the sun again. All this can come about through preaching. I know. I have seen it happen.

Let no one think that people want a sermon that is soft. They like it when it punches. "I don't want you to misunderstand what I am going to say," a woman said to me one day, "but we love you for the hell you give us!" I hadn't meant to "give 'em hell," but I knew what she meant. She meant what so many laymen have in mind when they say at the close of a morning service, "You preached that just for me. I needed it." She meant what another woman was expressing when she wrote that for the first time in her life the sermons she was hearing made a difference in the way she lived. She expected a sermon to do something more than soothe. She wanted to hear the kind of preaching that has the power to turn lives upside down. When it comes right down to it, that's what most laymen want.

And they can get it. Let me tell you how.

1. First, they must frankly recognize the power they have to make or break a preacher. The man in the pulpit tends to rise as high as the men and women in the pew expect him to. If they expect little, they will get little. If they are confused and don't know what they have a right to expect from their preacher, he will reflect that confusion. But if they are in the habit of hearing great preaching and make it clear that they recognize it and want it, their minister will feel the tug of their expectations and rise to meet them.

A sermon comes to life as a congregation responds. Unless you have had experience with it, you cannot imagine what a difference there can be in the same sermon when preached to two different congregations. In one case it may be alive, vital, penetrating, and in the other a dull, slow, hard drag. The preacher is the same and his prepared material is the same, but the congregation is different. The laymen in the pew have far more to do with whether a sermon is good than most of them have ever dreamed. There is an unspoken language which they communicate to the man in the pulpit. He feels it and responds.

Someone said of Queen Mary, grandmother of the present Queen of England, that she was always surrounded by people of character, not because she attracted such people in the first place but because she created character in whoever was around her. "One realizes slowly," her lady-in-waiting once said, "that only the best is good enough for her, and she inspires one to grow in capacity to give the best in return." This is the effect great laymen have on their minister. They *make* character in him. They inspire him to give his best.

2. The second way the layman can improve the pulpit output is to learn to distinguish between good preaching and bad preaching. If the layman really recognizes great

preaching when he hears it, and can tell the difference, for example, between a profound sermon and a delightful homily and is quick to spot the sermon that sounds good but says nothing; if he can tell when a man is really doing his best, and when he is getting by on his "sincerity," his lovable personality, or his glib tongue, then he is in a position to help make a great preacher out of his minister. He is in a position to do it because if he recognizes all these things, he at least knows what he is looking for, and a clear vision of the goal is the first prerequisite of any achievement.

3. This leads to the third thing the laymen can do. They can seek to understand what goes into the making of great preaching. "It's just a matter of getting some ideas and illustrations put together isn't it?" they might ask. The answer is, "Yes, I suppose so—in the same way that a skilled craftsman building a piece of furniture has nothing to do but nail some boards together." I am no cabinet-maker myself, but I watched a friend build a desk one summer and it wasn't a simple job. It took him a long time. He worked at it and did it right. If something didn't suit him, he pulled it apart and did it over again, and he worked for a smoothness of finish long after I thought it was surely smooth enough. I learned something in watching him. I learned that whether in building a sermon or a desk, the materials going into it must be chosen carefully, measurements must be exact, proportion right. Each element included must fit where it is placed, and it must be a thing of beauty whether viewed as a whole or examined piece by piece. And perhaps, most important of all, its creator must find personal fulfillment in the knowledge that he has done his best.

Laymen should know that a good sermon requires many hours of hard work. They should know that it involves intensive study, deep thought, careful writing and rewriting, and a long time in learning, if it is to be delivered with the ease and naturalness that the congregation appreciates. As a rule of thumb, a good sermon requires an hour in the writing for every minute in the preaching. This is in addition to the reading that is necessary before the writing begins. More laymen should know that. If they know something about the work that goes into the preparation of a sermon they can help their minister to give the task the time it needs.

4. Not only must the laymen come to appreciate what goes into the making of a sermon, but they must also realize how important preaching is to the real preacher. A lady once asked Dr. Joseph Parker what his hobby was. "Preaching!" he answered. "But I mean in addition to preaching," she said, and he replied, "Preaching, not but preaching; everything with me ministers to preaching!" It is that kind of personal and complete involvement in the proclamation of God's word that caused the people of his city to say of one early Christian preacher: "Better that Constantinople cease to be than that John Chrysostom should cease preaching." As laymen come to appreciate the seriousness with which a great preacher takes his preaching, they will begin to take it seriously too and will not lightly miss a Sunday service or tolerate disrespectful or flippant comments about the great event that preaching is.

5. The next thing the laymen can do to guarantee great preaching in their church is to see that their minister is given both the time and place for intensive study. In recent years there has been an unfortunate trend in the building of churches. The minister's study is usually too small, poorly designed to inspire creative thought, and badly located. It is set up as an office rather than a study and designed for administrative work and counseling rather than for the thoughtful preparation of sermons. It is usually near the areas of heaviest foot traffic and the busy rumble of the church office with its ringing phones and whirling mimeographs. This means death to preaching, and is clear evidence of the fact that the preacher's role as administrator has crowded out his function as preacher. The study should be large enough for a man to pace the floor

without getting dizzy. It should be remote from distracting sounds and sights, and its walls should be lined with bookshelves which, hopefully, the minister will keep busy with books. If laymen really want the great preaching they keep asking their bishop and district superintendent to guarantee they will get in their next man, let them take the initiative in providing the environment in which it is most likely to develop. And let them say to the new minister when he arrives, what Verne Orr, a distinguished Southern California Methodist layman, said in an address to young preachers: "Every sincere layman expects his minister to try harder to please God than the congregation. That necessitates much time for study and preparation. You are called to preach—you must be good at it—this is the first and highest gage of your success."

Clearly laymen want great preaching. Some men are naturally better at it than others, but no one will preach on a consistently high level without consistent time for study. The word "study" does not really convey the whole story, however. It's not like cramming for an examination or meeting the deadline for a term paper. What is needed is the kind of creative leisure that nourishes inspiration. André Gide once said that "nothing excellent can be done without leisure." However this may apply in other fields, it certainly is true of preaching.

Once laymen have come to realize that they cut off great preaching at its source when they fail to provide an adequate place or sufficient time for their minister's study, they should then take steps to see that the necessary "leisure" is provided. "Leisure" as we use the word here is to be distinguished from play or just goofing off. Edna Ferber, the famous novelist, said recently in an interview that a writer never has a vacation. "You can't turn your mind off," she said. "Everything you see, feel, hear, or do, you store away." In the same interview she explained that she had sold her 116-acre Connecticut estate and moved into a New York apartment because "I found the idea note pad

I kept on my bedside table was not reflecting my thoughts on life, which is my work. It was filled with 'See Oscar about the pump' or 'Find out if Fred will cut the hay.' So I lit out!" That says it for the preacher too. If he is a real preacher, his mind never takes a vacation from his job. But if he is loaded down with too many administrative and organizational responsibilities, his mind is forced to shift its attention to these things, with a consequent loss in the area of his special ministry.

6. The next thing the laymen can do follows from the previous items. They can take charge of the administrative details of the church so that the minister is relieved of the kind of pressures that so often reduce his study time to a minimum.

I know that is easier to agree to than to accomplish. Any minister who has been in the work for a while knows what it is to be told that he isn't expected to do much of the administrative work but is to concentrate on his sermons, and then discover that no arrangements, or at least no workable ones have been made to care for the administrative detail, so it all falls back on him whether anyone wants it that way or not. It is also true that most ministers get so accustomed to handling the administrative operations of the church that they don't know how to withdraw from them when they have the opportunity. In these instances the laymen should insist. Let there be no token gestures in the direction of taking over the tasks of general management, but let them either do it themselves as volunteers, or employ extra staff personnel to do it. This does not rob the minister of his rightful position at the head of the church organization. He will continue to be consulted with regard to all major matters, but he will be freed from the tyranny of administrative details.

7. The next thing the laymen can do to restore preaching to its former position of greatness is to stay out of the pulpit. That may sound negative, and it is, but it is important. In recent years, with increasing emphasis on the

role of the laity, people often suggest that a layman should be in the pulpit. Layman's Day is widely observed, and for most people it means the day a layman preaches the sermon. Sometimes the assignment is given to two or three laymen, who divide the sermon between them—a particularly gruesome sort of homiletical homicide. The same sort of thing may take place on a special Sunday for women or for youth. Frequently these laymen conduct the entire morning service.

This procedure is wrong. We ought to know that, because attendance generally falls off on the Sunday the laymen take over. Most laymen are no more enthusiastic about hearing another layman preach than asking a congenial friend, untrained in medicine, to remove their appendix.

Yet the practice continues. It seems to be based on the fallacy that the way to elevate the importance of the layman is to have him do the work of the clergy. Actually, this has the reverse of the desired effect. You don't make a person look big by having him do a job for which he is not trained. And you don't make a job seem important if you suggest it can be turned over to anyone whether trained or not. If preaching is of major importance, if a man needs to do three years of theological study beyond his four-year college degree to lay the groundwork for it, and spend twenty hours in the writing of a single sermon, it doesn't make sense to turn the job over to someone who has not trained for it at all.

Besides, to assume that the way to make the layman's job look important is to have him do what the minister is supposed to do is a way of saying that the layman really doesn't have much importance in his own right. I am unwilling to say that. The layman is the key unit in the life of the church and he doesn't have to pretend he is a preacher in order to give the illusion of being important.

8. One more objection to the use of laymen in the Sunday service is that very often they are brought in on special days in order to promote something. This ought not to be

done. It is misusing the hour of worship to turn it into a promotional venture.

If the laymen give the minister the idea that they want a chance at the pulpit, he will probably give it to them. But if they make it quite clear, as many great laymen I know do, that they do not wish to see the pulpit turned over to laymen even one day a year, he will get the idea that preaching is his job and he had better do it. Meanwhile the laymen have their work to do and should be busy with that.

Yet, at the risk of weakening what I have just said, I must make it clear that I am not presenting this idea as an absolute. The minister does not possess the pulpit. There are times when a layman should be there. At such times he should stand in his place with confidence and speak his piece without apology. For example, in the absence of an ordained minister, a dedicated and capable layman should conduct the service and preach the sermon. Or, again, when an outstanding layman has a special and powerful Christian message to present, the pulpit should be available to him. For example, if one of my members were the president of the National Council of Churches, I should be quick to invite him to speak to my congregation and his, some Sunday morning. However, these situations come in the category of exceptions that prove rather than negate the basic rule.

9. Another way in which the laymen can restore the prominence of the pulpit is to emphasize and safeguard the uniqueness of the Sunday morning service. I know churches where the laymen are quite willing to stay out of the pulpit in the sanctuary, but they set up little pulpits of their own in the adult Sunday-school classes. The classes operate like little churches with hymns, scripture reading, prayer, and "sermon" by the teacher. Some people belonging to these classes never attend the Sunday worship service in the sanctuary. "The Sunday-school class is my church," they say. That proves two things. First, that they have a false

concept of the function and importance of the Sunday worship service, and second, that they have a false concept of the function and importance of a church-school class. It is degrading to the whole principle of sound Christian education to turn classes into imitations of a church service. In a day when the learning process is being intensified in our schools and colleges and when adults by the thousands are registering for night school or correspondence courses, the church must bring its adult church-school classes up to standard. One hour a week is a brief enough time for them to do some solid work, and that hour should not be dissipated by announcements, sunshine committee reports about the sick and ailing, a special musical number of some kind, or a repetition of the elements of worship which they will go through all over again when they enter the sanctuary the next hour for the regular church service.

It is time our adult church-school classes reached their maturity. They should convene on time, open with a brief invocation, and launch into intensive study of the Christian faith and mission. That and that alone is their reason for existence. A solid hour of that kind of learning experience should prepare them to move from the classroom to the sanctuary to participate in corporate worship, and to respond meaningfully to great preaching.

As it stands now, many of the most enthusiastic boosters of their church-school class really do not want a church-school class at all. They don't want to study, they don't want to think, they don't want to learn. They want to meet with congenial friends under the auspices of the church, fill an hour with a kind of variety program that will keep them from getting bored, and enjoy the cozy feeling of belonging to such a wonderful group. Their weekly gathering, reminiscent of the rural church of their childhood, has almost no appeal to anyone for whom it has no particular nostalgic significance. This fact doesn't seem to bother them.

The responsibility of the sincere Christian layman should

therefore be quite clear. He should make certain that the adult church-school classes provide distinct and high quality educational experiences which complement rather than compete with the service of worship in the sanctuary.

10. Among all the steps the laymen can take to improve the preacher's preaching, none is more important than to guarantee him absolute freedom of the pulpit. He must preach what he is convinced is God's message to man or he is no preacher at all. If he is truly courageous, he will do this no matter what it costs him. But why test his courage, or force him to pay a greater price than is necessary? Rather, let the laymen share his daring. That is what they are doing when they defend his right to preach like a prophet.

In the last analysis, the preacher must be encouraged to approach his preaching the way Strunk and White say that the writer should approach his task. He must "please and satisfy himself," they say. He "always plays to an audience of one. Let him start sniffing the air, or glancing at the Trend Machine, and he is as good as dead, although he may make a nice living." Nothing could better express my conviction about preaching. The preacher preaches to himself. If he is honest in grappling with himself, he will be dealing with the basic human issues that are important to all men. But when he starts sampling opinion with the hope of preaching what is pleasing to his congregation, he is revealing his own impoverishment of soul, and opening the door to a new low of superficiality. When laymen sense their minister is doing this, let them make it clear to him that they want him to preach his own convictions not his idea of theirs. They want their pulpit to be a voice, not an echo, and they want the Sunday sermons to be prophetic utterances, not a weekly summary of informal opinion polls conducted by the preacher as he moves about the parish.

When I say that laymen must guarantee their minister freedom of the pulpit if he is to do great preaching, I do not mean to infer that he is so delicate that he must be dealt with more gently than others. It isn't that the preacher is so special that he must be protected and helped as though he were the king and the laymen his loyal subjects. Rather it is that Christ is special! God is special! The gospel is special! And the minister has been set aside as one called to bring Christ's gospel of God's kingdom through the high act of preaching. The true preacher knows himself to be nothing and God everything. By insisting on freedom of the pulpit, the laymen are simply doing what they can to make the pulpit a channel of God's grace.

11. The next thing the layman should do to lift the standard of preaching in his church is to sharpen his own skill in listening to a sermon. He should listen as a reporter would listen, asking himself, "What is the preacher saying? What is his main idea?" He should feel free to take notes on the sermon if he wishes to do so. Many people find this a good way to focus their attention on what is being said. It helps them remember the sermon, even if they never refer to their notes again. A good sermon has a clear-cut outline. The attentive listener learns to watch for it and to use it as a means of understanding all that the preacher is saying. The layman who listens to the sermon as a reporter would listen, is off to a good start.

The second way he should listen is as a philosopher. He should ask, "What is the *meaning* of what is being said? Are these ideas true? What other ideas follow from these?" The function of the sermon is not so much to *fill* the mind as to *stir the action* of the mind. The most important ideas in the sermon are not those spoken by the minister but those thought by the worshipers as they let their minds explore beyond where the sermon was able to go. The spoken sermon is not the big event in the service of worship. It is the invitation to the big event. The big event is what takes place inside the mind of each worshiper in response to the spoken sermon. One should listen to the sermon as a philosopher, following each idea out as far as his mind will take him.

He should also listen to the sermon as a counselee. He should ask, "How does this sermon apply to me? Does this sermon contain a prescription for my troubles? Is the minister speaking to me in a special way today?" As the layman listens to the preacher, the question in his mind should not be "How is he doing?" but "How am I doing?", just as one does not come to the doctor to examine the doctor's health, but his own.

One fine church woman said to me one day, "It always amazes me when I hear a good sermon, how many people I can think of who ought to be hearing it. It isn't until my enthusiasm for saving someone else cools off that it dawns on me the sermon is speaking pretty directly to me. I've also discovered that if I feel sensitive or defensive about something the minister has said, it is always to my benefit to discover why I feel that way." She has learned the art of making the act of listening to a sermon a genuine counseling experience. She listens to sermons with the expectation of being helped.

The fourth way a layman should listen to a sermon is as an executive. He should ask, "How can this sermon be put to work? Can I administer a plan for practicing what he preaches?" The layman should leave the church on Sunday morning not so much impressed with what happened *during* the hour he spent there as with what is going to happen *because* of the hour he spent there. He should emerge onto the street with a plan of action, and a determination to execute the plan. It may not always turn out right, but he will grow with experience, and he will always have the confidence Dwight L. Moody had when he answered a critic by saying, "At least, I like my way of doing it better than your way of not doing it."

When the preacher finds that his laymen are taking his preaching seriously enough to act on the basis of it, he will take it a good deal more seriously himself. The quality of his pulpit output will markedly improve.

The simple fact is that a sermon is a cooperative venture between minister and people. It is something they do together. To be effective, a preacher must give each sermon the very best he has—his best thinking, his best wording, his best speaking. Then he should pour himself into it and deliver, not a speech only, but his soul to the people. And each layman must bring his best to that joint experience of preacher and people which the sermon is. He must listen with full concentration, respond with his whole self, and act with courage and confidence. He should remember that a sermon is not finished when it has been preached. It has merely changed hands. That is what "delivering" a sermon means. Just as there is an art of preaching there is an art of practicing what is preached. And the latter art is the greater of the two.

VI

On Being a Literate Layman

Closely related to the act of preaching is the discipline of study. This is of paramount importance to the preacher as he prepares for the sermon. It is of no less significance for the layman as he responds to it. Study surrounds a good sermon, both undergirding it and emanating from it. That is why we must turn now to a consideration of the layman's pursuit of knowledge. This includes the study of theology, which was dealt with in Chapter III, but it involves much more.

The illiteracy to be found among church members is appalling. Many, perhaps most of them, know next to nothing about the Bible. They often misquote it, or quoting it correctly, misinterpret it. They have only the vaguest notion of what the Christian faith teaches, and are more inclined to conjure up a mixture of personal prejudices and old wives' tales and call the concoction the Christian faith than to learn what Christianity really is. On the whole, the

Christian church today is stronger in numbers than in knowledge. Noting that people say that "Christianity has gone almost dead in the modern mind," Charles W. Ranson, Dean of Drew University Theological School, observes that "the modern mind in which it has gone dead is, as often as not, inside the church."

That is not to say that church people are more illiterate than others. (Although, considering the Christian emphasis on the pursuit of truth, they have less excuse for being ignorant.) It is to say, however, that churchmen share with the rest of their generation the dubious distinction of being the most ignorant educated people any generation has produced. As Bishop Gerald Kennedy observes, "For a generation that prides itself on its realism, we can believe more things that are not so than a superstitious jungle tribe." Clifton Fadiman is just as hard on us. He says, "The average high school graduate today does not know who he is, where he is, or how he got there. He is lost." We are a nation of people who know how to read but prefer to look at pictures and, with immediate access to news of the world, are more interested in the comics than the front page. Our college graduates find it easier to pay their respects to education by subscribing to the alumni fund than by reading books. And church members are more likely to raise their pledge each year than to increase their religious knowledge.

Few laymen are bothered by their ignorance. J. B. Phillips says, "It is one of the curious phenomena of modern times that it is considered perfectly respectable to be abysmally ignorant of the Christian Faith." There is no shame in not knowing when ignorance is unavoidable but not to care whether one knows or not is a disgrace.

It leads to superficiality. It creates the kind of people Paul referred to as "talking without using [their] minds" (Phillips), or the kind you hear about who choose their books on the basis of color, to harmonize with the interior decoration of the room where they are to be placed. It encourages people to think that the only requirement for addressing an audience is a stubborn prejudice (usually called a conviction or point of view) and the nerve to stand up and talk. Such people wouldn't understand Bernard Baruch's assertion that "every man has a right to his opinion, but no man has a right to be wrong in his facts." Unfortunately there are always people around who will listen to them. John Wesley once said, "Let but a pert, self-sufficient animal, that has neither sense nor grace, bawl out something about Christ and his blood or justification by faith, and his hearers cry out, 'What a fine gospel sermon!'" Today it may not be the blood of Christ and "justification by faith" that are extolled, and it may not be for a "fine gospel sermon" that one is praised. But I have heard laymen with no theological understanding, knowledge of American history, or appreciation of the complex national and international scene recite some insipid platitude about "the Christian Spirit," or "true Americanism," and the dangers of the "welfare state," and have watched listeners nod approvingly to one another as though the most profound statement of the century had just been uttered. I have seen audiences break into enthusiastic applause for no other reason than that the speaker's prejudices corresponded with their own. The fact that what was being said didn't happen to be true concerned them not at all. How extreme this can be was illustrated by the comment one church woman made to my wife just after the Cuban crisis. The woman complained that President Kennedy had shown himself to be soft on Communism because he had not bombed Cuba to destroy Castro and his Russian visitors. My wife suggested that in all probability this would have led to world war and we might all have been destroyed. That prospect didn't worry the woman. "We would still come out ahead," she explained, "because after all, we have the resurrection!" And that woman is a college graduate, the wife of a professional man, an officer in the PTA and active in politics. She flies the American flag on holidays, attends her church on Sundays, and carries on a telephone barrage of reactionary propaganda on all days.

Fortunately there are few people like that either in or out of the church, but there are many like the college girl who walked away from a serious conversation saying, "I have to leave now. Thinking makes my head hurt." And there are plenty to fit Gustave Flaubert's description of Charles, in *Madame Bovary*. He said his "conversation was flat as a sidewalk, a place of passage for the ideas of everyman."

Jesus Christ came to bring truth. It would seem to follow, therefore, that no one should be more impatient with mental laziness or the careless handling of facts than Christian churchmen. Truth is our business and we had better be about it. Real churchmanship involves knowledge of the Bible, familiarity with the workings of one's denomination, awareness of the emerging world church, and an understanding of the meaning of the Christian faith for our highly technical and complex culture.

This is not surprising, since learning is naturally at the heart of the church. Jesus commended the pursuit of truth. The apostles encouraged study. St. Paul, not wanting to waste his time while in prison, sent for his books. Ancient monasteries were centers of learning. John Wesley was constantly urging his converts to read. It was the churches that founded the earliest universities in this country, and to this day they are among the first to break ground for new schools wherever they are needed. Most of the major denominations maintain large publishing houses and are continually seeking to upgrade the reading habits of the entire population. Surely St. Paul was speaking to us as well as to the Christians of the first century when he wrote, "My brothers, don't be like excitable children but use your intelligence! By all means be innocent as babes as far as evil is concerned, but where your minds are concerned be full-grown men!" (Phillips). Today more than ever before, the local church bears witness to the importance of learning with its abundance of modern classrooms and good literature, its well-stocked libraries and trained teachers.

Here then is our problem. In a day when unlimited knowledge is available but the taste for it has been dulled, what can we expect from Christian laymen with a heritage of sound learning, but slight experience of it? One thing at least is clear. They cannot win people to a faith they do not themselves understand. Speaking of our great American traditions, Max Ways, author of *Beyond Survival,* says, "We cannot carry a message that we have forgotten." Indeed we cannot. Christian laymen as well as American citizens have some remembering to do if they are to meet the challenge of massive ignorance in a day when true wisdom is both needed and available. How is this to be done?

The first step is to confess our ignorance. We are not likely to take significant strides toward increased knowledge until we recognize our lack of it.

The smartest people do. Charles Darwin once commented that all our knowledge "is something like an old hen's knowledge of a forty-acre field, in one corner of which she happens to be scratching." St. Paul confessed, "At present all I know is a little fraction of the truth . . ." (Phillips). John A. Hutton admitted, "There is always another side to the story. The great entertainment of Heaven for many a day will be, seeing the other side of a thousand things." Great minds recognize their limitations. One of the surest signs of an able thinker is his readiness to admit he might be wrong, and his acknowledgment of the fact that there is a mass of information he does not have.

Most of us are only vaguely aware of our need for more knowledge. We are sufficiently aware of it to apologize occasionally for our stupidity and to be easy marks for encyclopedia and great-books salesmen. We are sufficiently aware of it even to join a study class now and then in the hope that a group effort will accomplish what we failed to do alone. But we are not sufficiently aware of it to study the books we buy, or to stay with the class we join. A novelist, describing the home of a doctor, wrote, "There was a fir bookcase with six shelves, occupied almost exclusively by a set of the *Dictionary of the Medical Sciences,* its pages uncut but its binding battered by a long succession of owners." The longest intellectual step most of us have to take is the step between buying a book and reading it. Just about everybody these days will agree that serious study is important and that they ought to be doing more of it, but they act on the assumption that it is the least important claim on their time. They would think a person odd if he turned down a committee assignment so he would have more time to read books, but it doesn't seem to occur to them that if he doesn't read the books he won't have much of a contribution to make to the committee.

The problem is compounded by the mass of misinformation to which we are all subjected. Even the news dispatches we read, carrying the earmarks of authentic information, are frequently in error. William J. Lederer, in *A Nation of Sheep,* says: "The Associated Press, the night before Batista's flight, filed from Havana a dispatch which said that the rebel threat to Havana had 'faded in a storm of government firepower,' and that government troops 'hammered retreating rebel forces around Santa Clara tonight and drove them eastward out of Las Villas province.' Actually, Batista was preparing to flee. Castro was the victor."

It is easy to be mistaken. It is hard to be sure. That is why dogmatism is a stance unbecoming the Christian. We have been wrong too many times. More than once the church has stood squarely on the side of falsehood, and repeatedly, religious people have—in the name of their religion—propagated lies. Church people resisted the idea that the earth was round. And when Galileo and Copernicus proposed the theory that the earth rotated around the sun, a strong-minded churchman retorted, "The opinion of the earth's motion is of all heresies the most abominable, the most pernicious, the most scandalous, the immovability of the earth is thrice sacred; arguments against the immortality of the soul, the existence of God, and the incarnation, should be tolerated sooner than an argument to prove that the earth moves." In our own generation, ardent churchmen have authored state laws forbidding the teaching of evolution in the schools. They have opposed education in family planning, taught that the colored races were inherently inferior, confused a particularly offensive brand of "Americanism" with Christianity, and denounced their greatest leaders when they became controversial figures. Many Sunday-school children have been taught a narrow theology that has had to be painfully "unlearned" in college, and many a church has been more adept at adjusting its beliefs to fit the way of life to which its members had become addicted than at inspiring its members to exemplify its beliefs. Many a churchman, too sure of himself and the dependability of his own mind, has declared as a certainty that which should have been presented with a modest prefacing phrase like, "It seems to me . . ." Unfortunately, we seem slow to learn from our checkered history. I have noticed that those who are most critical of the church for its past and present inadequacies thunder their denunciations and warnings with more self-assurance than their conclusions warrant. It just may be that they don't have the final truth. They too are human. Somewhere their logic is erroneous. Some of their "facts" are bound to be found a little later not to be facts at all, and the bold conclusions they build on them will come tumbling down.

That's why it is so important for all churchmen to be humble. The church and even its greatest leaders have always been partly wrong. No matter how much we know, we are still desperately in need of more information about the Bible, church history, Christian doctrine, our own denomination, comparative religions, the ecumenical movement, theological trends, and the path of renewal through Christ for ourselves and for the world.

Yet knowledge alone is not enough. It must be knowledge of ultimate importance. It is possible that one may be able to give the scientific names of all flowers of the fields and yet not have enough insight to know that "Solomon in all his glory was not arrayed like one of these" (Matt. 6:29b) or that you and I "are of more value than they" (Matt. 6:26b). He may know mathematics and be able to produce a machine that can complete complicated calculations in a few seconds, and yet fail to comprehend that the widow's pennies add up to more than larger gifts deposited by less consecrated hands. He may be able to give a learned lecture on astronomy or geology or biology or some other aspect of *creation* and be tongue-tide when asked a simple question about the *Creator*. As Paul once put it, "Remember that there are men who have plenty to say, but have no knowledge of God" (Phillips). A person may have much knowledge without having the most important knowledge.

The second thing the layman must do to fight religious illiteracy is to examine the present educational structure of the church.

"Christian education" is a familiar term to modern Christians. We have our church schools, our curriculum materials, and top quality professional leadership. Yet, concerning the Christian faith, the laymen who pay for all these things remain largely uneducated. It seems incredible that at the precise point in church history when we have the best educational facilities, the widest knowledge of good teaching methods, the finest equipment and teaching aids, the most professionally prepared textbooks, and the finest methods of administration and supervision since Jesus told the disciples to go teach the gospel, that we should have what is surely an all-time low in percentage of Christians who have any clear concept of what the gospel is.

There are reasons for this. Here are some of them:

1. Many Christian educators are more enamored of modern pedagogy than they are committed to ancient truths. They swoon over exciting new methods of learning, forget-

ting that there is more teaching power in a life committed to Christ than in all the methods described in educational journals. They are long on technique and short on conviction.

As with other modern educators, they may be more stimulated by interesting ways of communicating the truth than dependable ways of knowing it. They like to "arouse interest," "stimulate attention," and employ each exciting technique of group dynamics or audio-visuals. The dangers involved in such a trend are sighted by Joseph Wood Krutch when he writes:

> What so many enthusiasts of communication will not realize is that there is a point beyond which everything should not be made varied, vivid, picturesque, dramatic, and "interesting." A time is sure to come when something which needs very much to be learned cannot possibly be made as vivid, picturesque, dramatic, and interesting as certain other things. And when that time comes, only the individual who can turn his attention to what is most important, rather than allow it to be captured by what is most interesting, is capable of being educated. A population entrusted with the power to make decisions but incapable of sustained attention is in a parlous condition.[1]

Krutch's warning was not directed at the church, but it applies to it. Our gospel is too important to be lost in clever methodology.

2. Advanced courses are almost unheard of in the local church, and scarcely anyone progresses beyond the elementary level. While a college has academic standards for admission and many courses cannot be taken until one has completed certain others that are prerequisite to them, educational opportunities in the church are open to all. If you

[1] *Human Nature and the Human Condition* (New York: Random House, 1959), pp. 136–137.

are fifteen years old and register for the first time in the church school, you are put in the tenth-grade class with youngsters who have attended all their lives, without anyone's raising a question as to whether you will be out of your depth competing with those who have been in the church school since nursery days. The tragedy is that you probably won't be.

3. Intensive application of one's mind to the subject matter is not required. No intellectual demands are made of the students. There are no examinations to stimulate intensive review and no term papers requiring independent study. Disciplined learning is not insisted upon and students are neither shamed nor shaken out of the muddleheadedness that is born of lethargy.

4. As was noted in Chapter V, too little attention is given to sermon preparation and too many preachers fail to take the pulpit's teaching opportunity seriously. The result is that the best opportunity the church has to challenge Christians to serious study and vigorous thought, as well as to give them an example of what it looks like in action is missed.

5. There is a tendency to associate Christian education with children. Nearly always when appeals are made in behalf of the church's educational program, the emphasis is on "doing something for our children." Youth have a share in it too, but here the image is that of week-end camping, Friday night dances, and a lounge where they can meet their friends in a safe atmosphere.

Meanwhile, adult classes, if they are held, exist more for their social value than the learning opportunity they afford. The "coming attractions" for the adult groups of one church, as reflected in a single issue of its parish paper, invited participation in an evening of "entertainment" provided by a traveling shutterbug who would show pictures of his latest trip, an all day outing to a nearby lake, a "Fun Night for Grown Ups," an ice-cream social, a Family Frolic for parents (planned and carried out by their children), several picnics, two tours, a pancake breakfast, two garden parties, a home talent show, and a Family Camp advertised as an "inexpensive holiday" (although in the last sentence it was admitted that discussion and worship would have a place on the program along with recreation). Here is *involvement* with a capital "I." It is also *fiddling* with a capital "F" while the world *burns* with a capital "B."

6. In a world of public relations experts and advertising gimmicks, the sales pitch, and the lure of affluence, Christian education is up against some stiff competition. As a "felt need," it is usually secondary to the study of investments, interior decoration, sports, and other blocks of specialized knowledge that are more obviously related to this wonder-world that modern science has set us in.

The Christian layman needs to take a hard look at modern religious education, identifying its strengths without evading its weaknesses. Aroused concern will lead to next steps. One of the first will be to fill in the gaps in his own religious knowledge. It is encouraging to report that many laymen are doing just that. The world-wide rise of the laity is characterized by a demand for knowledge. Most of the people involved in the movement, however, are bypassing the traditional adult departments of church schools. This may be too hasty. Not all of the traditional Sunday-school classes, woman's society study groups, and men's clubs are to be dismissed as superficial or irrelevant. For the most part, their lesson materials and study books are prepared by excellent writers with a sound theological background. They are both Biblically based and currently relevant. Their greatest variable has been in the quality of teaching provided, but this is the variable with which all educational ventures must struggle. The truth is that some adult Sunday-school classes and teachers would do credit to any theological seminary, and some church men's groups have moved beyond the level of service-club levity to sound Christian study and action. And the woman's societies of our churches, often dismissed by the ignorant as "sewing circles," and frequently appealed to for some of the money they always seem to have more of than anybody else, have done as much as anyone in Protestantism to quicken the conscience and inform the mind of the church concerning the great social issues of our time.

Meanwhile, the new thrust toward greater intellectual respectability in the lay movement has defects and problems of its own. Its tendency to discredit the immediate past is juvenile. Its disdain for other and more humble approaches to the Christian life is arrogant. And its emphasis on intellectual soundness, while overdue among the laity, carries the seeds of spiritual sterility. Too many of its enthusiasts forget that it is the child of the institutionalized church and its future is closely related to it.

In any event, the awakened laymen, with a new awareness of the need for Christians to hold up one another's hands, should give solid support to those seeking to develop a sound program of Christian education. To be sure, some of the theories under which they have operated have been wrong, but who among us has operated under theories that are 100 per cent defensible? Taken as a group, the persons engaged in the work of Christian education in the local church are as intelligent, purposive, and self-sacrificing as any in the organization. I always enjoy speaking at annual Christian education dinners because I know that the audience will be perceptive, responsive, friendly, and deeply committed to the Christian faith. While much that these people are involved in needs improvement, many of the deficiencies are the result of seemingly necessary compromise between what they would like to do and what the limited vision of the rank and file membership of the church permits them to do. The informed layman will do all he can to give these people the support they deserve. This is a good deal more respectable behavior than to declare the institutionalized church to be beyond renewal, turn tail and run. The world may be beyond renewal too, but some of us plan to stick with it.

Besides confessing his ignorance and giving support to a strong church program of Christian education, the layman who wants to fight religious illiteracy will commit himself to personal disciplines appropriate to a true intellectual.

One morning I sat at the breakfast table with ten laymen whom I had invited to my home to discuss the meaning of the Christian faith for our lives and for the world. They were among the top leaders in our church and in their respective vocations. To start the meeting I asked each man to tell briefly the story of his own spiritual pilgrimage. It was a great experience. The stories were authentic. The men were honest. Each brief autobiography was unique. These men wanted a deeper experience of religion than they had found up to this time, but they were frank to say that they did not expect to find it in a Sunday-school class or a church-fellowship group. They would as soon have joined a ladies' circle or the nursery department as to get caught in one of those spiritual-life or prayer groups they had often heard about. Clearly they wanted the deeper understanding of Christianity that these groups claimed to give, but their previous experiences with them had not led them to believe that the advertised merchandise was likely to be delivered. They wanted something more vigorous and manly.

I shall never forget what one of the men, a leading heart surgeon, had to say. His opening words were, "I am a mediocre Christian." That didn't seem at all appropriate to me since I considered him to be one of the finest Christian gentlemen I knew. But he continued: "If a man wants to be an outstanding surgeon he must discipline himself for it. He must get up earlier than the other fellow and work harder. When he runs into a puzzling problem he must take the time and consume the energy it takes to find the answer. He must seek to improve his technique and find opportunities to observe the work of others from whom he can learn. I have done that. I have refused to settle for mediocrity in surgery. But I have settled for mediocrity in Christianity. I have gone to church all my life. We take our children to Sunday school and assume some church responsibilities ourselves. We are a church family. But my participation in all of this is on the level of the doctor who is willing to settle for mediocrity in his profession. I am a mediocre Christian. I never realized that until now. But in the future I want to study the Christian faith and live the Christian life with the same kind of dedication I give to surgery."

That is exactly what he has done in the days since that first meeting. He makes no fuss about it. He just does it, and in doing it he has set a standard of Christian discipline in study and action which has inspired me to rejuvinate my own tired disciplines, tighten my spiritual muscles, improve my study habits, and reclaim the vigor and zest of the Christian life.

Unfortunately, however, comparatively few laymen recognize the mediocrity of their particular brand of Christian living. And few of those who are aware of it do anything to correct the deficiency. They modernize their houses and update their business practices while seeking to satisfy their spiritual needs with the smatterings of Biblical knowledge picked up in their childhood. It has never occurred to some of them that Christianity demands intellectual vigor. To them it requires nothing but a kindly disposition to show goodwill toward their fellow man. But as Martin E. Marty puts it, "good will is not enough by itself; it is not enough unless it is coupled with some historical understanding, some theoretical application, and some technical awareness."

It is not easy to discipline oneself for a life of study and growth in the faith. Most of us need some built-in reminders. I have three small wood carvings in my study which, along with my book-lined shelves, remind me that I must be relentless in my pursuit of knowledge. Two of the carvings are of robed priests whose eyes are fixed on the open pages of the scripture. The other is called "The Bookworm." Brought to me from Heidelberg by a friend who said it reminded him of me, it is a carving of an emaciated little old man standing on one book, holding another in one hand, and a third, which he is reading, in the other, while two additional books are clamped respectively under his left arm and between his knees. His thirst for knowledge is an inspiration to me, but there is nothing to indicate what he is reading. It isn't enough to be a "bookworm." One must read what is important.

Which brings us to the fourth suggestion for the layman concerned about the church's approach to learning. He must remember that knowledge alone is not enough. Important knowledge is the goal. No one can read everything that is available. That's why it is so important to be selective. We must recognize that among things that are important to know, some are worthy of more intensive study than others. Thus we shall have made a great stride forward when in school and church school we are as eager for our children and youth to gain a knowledge of God and the power of his love as we are for them to know all the facts about sex; when we are as eager to familiarize them with the language of the saints as we are to expose them to the language of the gutter. I do not believe in censorship. I do not think young minds should be shielded from knowledge of the existence of the ugly and the sordid. But I am convinced that not all knowledge is of equal importance and that whatever it is that dominates our attention will, in due course, dominate us. Jesus once told the intellectual leaders of his time that they had given too much attention to the superficial and too little attention to what he called the "weightier matters" (Matt. 23:23). And Paul once enumerated whatever is true, honorable, just, pure, lovely, gracious, whatever is excellent and worthy of praise and said bluntly "*think* about *these* things" (Phil. 4:8). The Christian faith combines spiritual aspiration with intellectual striving. It is a faith based on knowledge, and knowledge selected in faith.

That brings us to the fifth thing one must do if he is to be a literate layman. He must get his emotions involved.

It is true, of course, that strong emotion can black out reason. Nothing has done more to give the church a bad name among intelligent people than the emotional excesses of zealous Christians. A scientifically oriented generation is especially impatient with this kind of thing. However, there is nothing new about it. Noting that many people have a commitment to God that is worthless because it is senseless, Paul said of one group, "I know from experience what a passion for God they have, but alas, it is not a passion based on knowledge" (Phillips). That describes a good many people in our churches. They have a religious passion in an intellectual vacuum. With a maximum of emotion and a minimum of reason they have been poor representatives of the Christian faith.

Nevertheless, to recognize that emotion may be dished up in too generous a measure is not to say that the alternative is to eliminate it in favor of pure reason. Indeed, there is good ground for supposing that one extreme is as bad as the other and that reason untouched by emotion is no nearer truth than emotion that disregards reason. In suggesting that we *love* God with our *minds*, Jesus seems to have linked them together. If there is such a thing as "pure reason," it must be reason purified by constructive emotion. Otherwise it is likely to be found to be *un*reasonable. There is some knowledge that is understandable to the mind only if it has passed through the heart. Coleridge once said that "deep thinking is obtainable only by a man of deep feeling." And Shakespeare in *A Midsummer Night's Dream* gives credit to the emotions of lovers and madmen for the capacity to understand "more than cool reason ever comprehends."

If we are to increase our knowledge, and use it effectively, we must develop a passion for it. Anything worth doing requires fervor for its accomplishment. Thoreau expressed it well, back in 1851, when he said, "The intellect is powerless to express thought without the aid of the heart . . ." And more recently, Webb Garrison, author of *Creative*

Imagination in Preaching, called attention to the close relationship between reason and emotion when he wrote: "After solving a difficult problem, Sir Isaac Newton was often filled with such ecstasy that he had to stop work for a time. Revelations that led to discovery of analytic geometry left Descartes in a state of 'radiant enthusiasm.' Spinoza's intuitions, which led to many of his philosophical views, were accompanied by feeling so intense he could describe it only as 'a sense of glory.'" And Garrison adds, "Perhaps the pleasure that accompanies insight stems from man's recognition that thinking a new thought is his most sublime achievement."

We must be emotionally committed to the truth or we will never get it. We must want truth more than we want peace of mind, or a square meal, or a new car, or popularity, or even unity and goodwill. Truth is basic, and any civilization that is not built on it will crumble; any personality that is not devoted to it will decay. Albert Schweitzer once wrote, "I think the most important quality of a person concerned with religion is resolute devotion to the truth." Devotion has an emotional quality.

It involves love. This brings us very close to the heart of the Christian faith. No matter how much we intellectualize it, I suspect that about 99 per cent of us, if asked to define Christianity would say something about love. Jesus said that the great commandment is to love God and our fellow man, and Paul and the apostles continually reminded the early Christians to love one another.

We have said that the Christian faith is based on knowledge, and that is true. But knowledge without love is as dead as bones not clothed in flesh. Paul reminds us that "while knowledge may make a man look big, it is only love that can make him grow to his full stature" (Phillips). Scientific objectivity is important, and I would defend it to the end, but scientific accuracy is no substitute for warmth of feeling. Intellectual capacity is of little value without humaneness of spirit. Intelligence divorced from love leads to bestiality. That is why Howard Thurman can write, with his usual perceptiveness, "There is only one place of refuge on this planet for any man—that is in another man's heart." Knowledge we must have, but knowledge interpreted by love.

Albert Schweitzer personified this combination. He was a thinker. No one would challenge, and few could match, his intellectual ability. He had doctorates in medicine, philosophy, music, and theology. Yet he chose to use his knowledge in loving service to uneducated and underprivileged people. It is told of him that one day when they were cutting and rolling logs for building the hospital at Lambaréné, a native villager passed by, neatly dressed in white shirt and pants. Schweitzer called to him to lend a hand with the logging, but the man replied, "I cannot help you. Can you not see I'm an intellectual!" And Dr. Schweitzer replied, "Yes, I see. I, too, once wanted to be an intellectual; but didn't make it."

What the church needs is more laymen who, in Schweitzer's words, wanted to be intellectuals but didn't make it. Or, more precisely, men and women who think clearly and act lovingly.

They are in short supply. It isn't that our churches do not have plenty of members who are smart, and plenty who do kind things, but even these people, when caught up in the activities of the church often lose their usual good sense. They feel smothered by layers of traditions they only vaguely understand, and blocked by the religious suppositions of the other members. What is needed is for them to apply as much hard-headedness to their church as to their business. They must ask questions, challenge assertions, demand proof, and express distaste for innocuous social functions, poorly run meetings, and sentimentality in handling personnel problems. They must challenge the double-talk they hear when members seek to justify racial exclusiveness with the Christian gospel. When such an assertion describes the facts, they must tell their men's club that the reason they don't attend meetings is that the latter are nothing but inferior reproductions of the community's service clubs and do nothing to further the real work of the church. They must notify the women that their gossiping will not be tolerated, that they can live up to higher standards than that, and they must direct their department of Christian education to do a respectable job of sound educating.

Literate laymen know that the business of the Christian church is the Christian faith. So simple and absolute is that truth that if the church's official board, Sunday-school classes, fellowship groups, or worship services are not obviously and constructively, constantly and almost obsessively at this business, then they are not the Christian church at all and have no right claiming to be.

Let the literate layman, knowing what the Christian faith really is and affirming his own dedication to it, notify every organized group in the church that they are not great, they are not Christian, they are not even important merely because they are a wonderful fellowship. Fellowship is not a distinctively Christian word. Where Christianity is at work, fellowship is broken as often as it is created. Jesus pointed out that even thieves and sinners have a nice relationship with each other. That isn't the test of Christianity at all and the sooner church members get wise to themselves and outgrow their obsession with fellowship groups, the sooner they will become the church. If they have good fellowship, they can be thankful for that, but it is not what they are in business for.

It is not enough for them to ease their consciences by taking on a service project of some sort, or to prove their religiosity by having a regular "devotional" before their meetings. The very fact that they tack on the devotional as a kind of duty, and look for a project to prove they have the service motive shows how far they are from being a Christian organization. If they are the church, they will worship from inner compulsion as inevitably as a spring gushes from the ground, and they will be at all times about their Father's business of serving others.

So let the literate laymen, with a fresh understanding of Christianity, insist that the groups in the church must not *have* worship and *take on* service projects. They must simply *be* disciples of Jesus Christ; then worship and service will be as natural as eating.

What does all that mean? It means a radically changed church. For one group it means to meet at their usual time and after a brief prayer for God's guidance, to go from door to door in the vicinity of the church, talking with people about the Christian faith and the church they represent. It means bringing new friends to the regular worship services of the church. For another group it means contacting every business and professional man in the area, every employee, to let them know the church is there and has a purpose. For another group it may mean getting a list of the shut-ins, finding out their particular needs, and organizing to meet them. Another group may organize to bring the Christian ethic to bear upon the political structure of the city. Another group will tackle the race problem at the point where it is closest to them. The list of possibilities is endless, but this much is clear: If they are a Christian group, they will not get together just because they like to get together. They will get together because they can serve the God of their Christ more effectively by cooperating with one another in an organized endeavor than by going it alone. In the process they will have the most satisfying fellowship they have ever experienced, but the fellowship will be the by-product, not the purpose.

If a few laymen catch the vision, others will see it too, and the church will regain its lost vigor. It will become for many what it is for a friend of ours who wrote to us:

> I've never been to college, but I think of the church as my alma mater. Assuming responsibilities in the Church school and in the women's work drove me to do

> reading and studying I'm sure I would never have done otherwise. I feel I've been given a liberal education including Theology, Sociology, History, Geography, Political Science and Literature. I received help in family life, and child care and there were even opportunities for developing some skills in office work. Not only does the Christian Church inspire her members to become intelligent and articulate citizens of the world, she trains them for the role.

What a testimony! I want to testify that that woman, without her college education, is one of the best informed and most mature persons I know. Her life is a symphony of good judgment, worthy purpose, and endless service.

St. Paul gave the right challenge: "Live life, then, with a due sense of responsibility, not as men who do not know the meaning and purpose of life, but as those who do. Make the best use of your time, despite all the difficulties of these days. Don't be vague but firmly grasp what you know to be the will of God" (Phillips).

Those are strong words, and good counsel for today's laymen.

A well-known football dictum states, "Never run with the ball before you've caught it." Church folks do a lot of running. They are forever going to this and going to that. But too few have caught the ball. Let them all lay hold of the fundamental truths of our faith, and carry them—against whatever opposition may arise—straight to the goal.

VII

Life in the Church Family

Pursuing truth, our paths converge. People seeking important knowledge find each other. As the layman continues his study and strives to build a sound educational program in his church so that all have a maximum opportunity to "increase in wisdom," he will find more than facts. He will find people. That is what this chapter is about.

It is about the layman's relationship to the church staff and the membership as a whole. They are his family. Jesus called his followers his "brother, and sister, and mother" (Matt. 12:50). Christians have often been called "the brethren," and the church "the household of God."

From the beginning, Christians have found the idea of the church being a family a particularly satisfying concept. Howard Grimes describes the meaning of it simply and well:

> For one who has known the close associations, the ties of love, the estrangement and reconciliation, the sin

> and forgiveness which characterize a good family, the Church may easily be seen as the larger "family of God." One is born into a family by biological birth through no act or choice of his own, as he is born into the Church by baptism. He must be cared for as an infant and child by the family, just as the Church, as a helper to the family, must nurture its children. Eventually a member of a human family must begin to assume for himself certain responsibilities, and finally he is put on his own but with his family as a continued source of aid. So the child must begin to assume responsibility for himself as he is able, and eventually he must become a fully convenanting member of the Church, accepting responsibility for his own acts. A child may become a prodigal son of his human family, just as he may also become a prodigal son of the Church. Yet he still "belongs" to his family, just as he still "belongs" to the Church. The family develops its unity as individual members interact with one another in estrangement and reconciliation, in sin and forgiveness, just as members of the Church, under Christ, must work out the manner in which their unity in Christ is implemented.[1]

Members of the church staff are part of the family. The layman should learn to know them and to relate intelligently to them.

The most common mental image of the church, except when it is thought of as a building, is *a minister and his "flock."* Actually, many churches have a multiple staff. With increased urbanization and the emergence of larger churches, a majority of today's laymen are related to congregations with more than one person on the pay roll. Many have two or more ministers. It is no longer unusual for as many as thirty or forty people to be employees of a single local church.

[1] *The Rebirth of the Laity* (Nashville: Abingdon Press, 1962), p. 32.

This change in the facts of the case has not been reflected in a corresponding shift in the layman's way of thinking. He still refers to "my pastor," meaning the senior minister, as though the other three or four ordained men on the staff were not important enough to be mentioned.

It is hard to define the exact relationship laymen and staff should have to one another. Actually, the staff are at once the members' employees and their leaders. Their work should be directed in accordance with the best principles of employer-employee relationships, and their leadership should be followed with loyalty and respect. In this kind of situation, the *spirit* of the relationship becomes the key factor. Where there is goodwill and unswerving loyalty to a common goal, lines of authority—while important—are not so likely to be crucial.

The existence of the right spirit among members of the congregation is often the factor determining success in the staff. When staff relationships are stormy, we usually look for the trouble within the staff itself, and point to a dominant senior minister or a disloyal subordinate. But the problem may stem from the members. The role of the congregation in building and maintaining good staff relationships receives too little notice.

Consider the economic factor. One day when I was trying to impress my children with the value of money and their good fortune in having what I thought to be a reasonably generous allowance, my clincher was to say that about the only money I could remember my parents having given me was when they lined the children up each Sunday morning and doled out two pennies apiece to put in the Sunday-school offering. My daughter responded, "Now I see why you went into the ministry, Dad. You thought there was money in it."

Few people choose church vocations as a means of satisfying inflated financial ambitions. Most of them could make more money in other employment. That is not to say that they are spiritualized beyond the need for adequate monetary compensation. Every staff member should receive an appropriate salary, and the church members should see that he does. That they fail to do this is evidenced by the number of times church employees resign to take jobs that are less attractive to them but with salaries that enable them to pay their bills. It is evidenced by the frequency with which a new minister is paid more than his predecessor because the hiring committee can find no suitable candidate who will come for what they had been paying. It is evidenced by the infrequency with which a raise in salary shows up in the church budget although the cost of living rises daily. It is evidenced by the helpless "We didn't know he wasn't satisfied with what he was getting" that is always heard when a faithful employee, in final desperation, asks for a raise. It is evidenced by the alarming increase in the number of ministers who have accepted part-time employment beyond the work of the church and by the number of ministers' wives who are employed. It is evidenced by an exaggerated emphasis some ministers are placing on wedding and funeral fees. Church positions are not expected to be economic plums, but compensation should always be a respectable measure of the quality of work desired, and it should be sufficiently generous to contribute to the employee's self-respect. The work of God's church will not be done effectively by money-mad ministers. All of us know that. No one has much respect for a man of the cloth for whom economics is the primary consideration. But it is equally true, though less well known, that God's work will not be done effectively by laymen who parcel out economic reward to their church employees on the basis of the minimum amount they can pay and still get the man they want. The church will never rise to its full stature as long as it operates on the fiction that Christianity requires a deeper dedication and greater financial sacrifices from those who are employed within the institution of the church than from those who as engineers, pilots, business executives, plumbers, doctors, lawyers, actors, and astronauts do the field work of the church by representing Christ in the places of their employment.

Nothing saps the strength of a church like dissension within the staff; nothing demoralizes a staff faster than a feeling that their work is not appreciated by the laymen; and, human though it may be, there is no more certain evidence of being appreciated than a good beginning salary with generous and frequent raises. This is a job for the laymen. No member of the staff, not even the senior minister in behalf of those who work under his administration, can handle this matter adequately. The laymen must do it.

Salaries are not all that need attention. Staff members share with the rest of the human family the need to be loved, to have their work praised, and to be reassured that their efforts are worth while. So, while shoddy work is not to be encouraged, egocentricity fed, or personal offensiveness tolerated, each employee's work should be recognized as important and his special accomplishments noticed and appreciated. Along with adequate monetary compensation, this special attention given to each one's field of service is the easiest and yet psychologically most supportive thing a layman can do for the members of the church staff.

In cases where a staff member's work cannot receive one's honest support, and especially where a change is needed and perhaps long overdue, the layman is faced with his greatest temptation to act irresponsibly. Many a church has been split over divided loyalties and conflicting counsel concerning the best way to handle personnel matters packed with high emotional potential. In such circumstances every conscientious churchman should follow these simple rules:

1. Familiarize yourself with your denomination's established procedures in such matters, and adhere strictly to them. These vary a great deal, and much unhappiness could be avoided if laymen would not bring Methodist assumptions to a Baptist ministerial problem or expect to call an Episcopal minister to his post after the manner of

the Congregationalists. Each system has its advantages and its shortcomings, and the temptation is to covet the other denomination's way of doing things when one's own church is caught with a serious problem.

2. Leave critical matters concerning personnel strictly in the hands of the administrator or church committee who has been authorized to handle them. Give these persons information you feel they should have, or your counsel if they seek it. But, however much restraint it may require, leave them alone. Don't complicate their problems by being one of their problems. Heated demands, accusations, or threats are never helpful, often inflammatory, and always unfair. They bring harm to everyone, even those they are designed to help. The stain of them sticks to a church for years.

3. Pray for all who are involved. Wise and fair decisions are easier to come by in an atmosphere of prayerful goodwill.

4. Where unministerial behavior or personal actions unbecoming a church employee are involved or suspected, be kind, remembering that human weakness is universal and that every indiscreet word or act has at least an explanation if not an excuse. Cooperate in finding solutions that are redemptive rather than destructive. Keep in mind that the church must maintain high standards of personal behavior, but refrain from being judgmental or unforgiving. When wise church officials seek to make a necessary shift in personnel as quietly as possible for the protection of reputations or to prevent unnecessary hurt to innocently involved persons, don't be the suspicious type, quick to think someone is being mistreated. Don't demand reasons for the dismissal. Much harm has been done by laymen who have forced what should have remained the knowledge of only a few into the open forum of public debate or even into the press.

Staff members will make their mistakes—sometimes serious ones, sometimes insignificant ones made serious as others choose to magnify them. Mature lay people can assimilate these normal inadequacies with ease as they acknowledge the sinfulness of all humanity. Robert Rodenmayer, an Episcopal clergyman, has the right attitude. He says, "A former curate of mine wrote to me after a number of years and said he was now aware of the fact that when he was my curate he had spent quite a bit of time stumbling over his own ego. In my reply I could only say to him that years ago I had written a similar letter and that during his curacy I might have been more useful to him if I had been more grown up myself." As I look back on a few experiences of strained staff relationships in my own ministry, I am inclined to view them in the same light. I did not then and I do not now defend the actions of the staff members involved, but I can understand and forgive them, and wish I had been more mature myself.

Meanwhile, let the laymen remember that they are partners with the staff in a common enterprise. No matter how many people the church employs to do its work, there is still more to be done than can get done, and the Christian layman will lift his share of the load rather than adding his weight to it.

He will also help to keep the total ministry of the church unified and operating with smooth orientation to the church's central purpose. Whether the ministerial staff consists of one man or five, the total task is the same. Although a church has several ministers, it has but one ministry. The present trend toward specialization in which men are trained as ministers of education, ministers of counseling and the like, must not become a trend toward fragmentation, dividing the church into specialized constituencies. An ordained clergyman is a minister first and a specialist second. His commitment is to the total church and its total mission. The layman's commitment should be the same.

This commitment to a central loyalty not only precludes actions which tend to divide the church into self-contained specialties but also prevents the more devastating divisions based on personal loyalties to individual ministers. Laymen should know that ministers have ambitions and are capable of professional jealousies. Through their Christian commitment they normally keep these under control. However, like other human passions, they can be stimulated. Nothing stimulates them faster than for laymen to talk to one minister about the shortcomings of another, to choose one in preference to another for a wedding ceremony or funeral service, or to reject a pastoral call as second-class treatment unless it comes from the senior minister. It is humiliating to competent clergymen to be rejected in favor of someone else; it is an insult to the Christian ministry to reduce it to a personality cult; and it is a waste of valuable staff time to duplicate services to individuals.

Therefore, while safeguarding the integrity of the various specialties and recognizing the administrative authority of the senior minister, laymen should avoid two temptations: the temptation to turn to the senior minister first for all sacraments and special services, accepting his colleagues on the staff only as substitutes, and the temptation to turn these sacred ceremonies into a popularity contest.

It is right that the senior minister should do most of the preaching. That is his specialty, and it was for this more than any other one thing that he was employed. When other ministers on the staff deliver the Sunday sermon, they are his substitutes just as he is their substitute when stepping in to cover the work in their area of specialization when they are sick or on vacation. But weddings, baptisms, funerals, confirmation, and the sacrament of the Lord's Supper are priestly functions of the total ministry and should be shared freely and without discrimination among the members of the ministerial staff. These are not the exclusive prerogative of the senior minister.

More important than sharing them freely is assigning them on some basis other than personality preference. When I went to one church I was told that it was the custom to hold a special service of infant baptism on Easter Sunday afternoon. All of the ministers on the staff were to be present, and parents of infants and small children were to choose which minister they wanted to administer the sacrament to their child. I was shocked. Normally when I go to a new church, I live with the traditions and practices I inherit until I experience them first hand and can evaluate their meaning and effectiveness. This was an exception. I was not about to reduce the holy sacrament of baptism to a spiritual beauty contest featuring the clergy. I do not know how the custom got started and I never bothered to find out. I was satisfied to bring it to a quick and quiet end.

Another portion of the church family whom the layman should come to know and love is made up of all his fellow members. Neither knowing nor loving them will be easy. Just getting acquainted requires one to go where people are and to learn their names. Really knowing them involves much more. It involves meaningful conversation, willingness to share deeply of oneself, and cooperation in some joint endeavor. As for loving one's fellow church members, the challenge is as wide as the list of human antagonisms.

Living as we do in a competitive world where, in wit, wisdom, and wealth, people seek to gain advantage over one another, it would be surprising if something of this same spirit were not found in the church. We can hardly expect laymen to outbargain their business associates, outrank their fellow professors, and outwit their friends and neighbors every day but Sunday. On the contrary, the spirit of competition accompanies them to the house of worship. Many laymen compete with one another for recognition and position. This is natural enough because a church is a brotherhood. Brothers and sisters are "siblings." Sibling rivalry is a well-known human condition. In the church family it may be competition for office or reputation or the best pie at the potluck. Even the newcomer is thrust almost at once into the competitive situation. When he complains, "No one spoke to me," he is saying, "I failed in my bid for attention. Others were noticed, but not I." This is relatively simple and harmless, but when the rivalry resolves itself into a long-time struggle for power between competing groups or individuals it can become an ugly thing.

When the power is no longer struggled for but is firmly held by some individual or group, it is just as bad. Power and insensitivity to the feelings of others tend to go together. We see this in the world of political dictatorships. It is said that during the Syrian campaign, Napoleon "ordered twelve hundred prisoners of war shot because they were an encumbrance." He once said to Prince Metternich, "A man like me does not care a damn for a million lives." I have never seen anyone in church who put that low a price tag on his brother Christians, but I have seen some of them act with high-handed disregard for the other fellow's feelings and rights.

Power-possessing people are not the only ones who do this, however. Some of the meanest things that are said and done in church life originate with people who once had power but have lost it, as for example those who are rotated off an important committee. Speaking of what he calls "downward mobility" in professional or economic status, Vance Packard discusses people who, for one reason or another, have had to step out of the limelight, or take a cut in salary. He says they frequently suffer prolonged emotional upsets, and adds:

> Many socially declining or downward-mobile people turn to alcohol or drugs for support. Some become promiscuous. They often become known as troublemakers, with chips on their shoulders. Even their best friends become perplexed as to how to approach them without being snarled at. Wives find them disagreeable as mates. Such declining males are gloom-ridden, and those becoming seriously disturbed emotionally tend to develop sadistic-masochistic (destructive or self-destructive) attitudes. Two studies agree that the down-

ward-mobile people who are referred to psychiatrists are among the most difficult of all types to aid. They rebuff the psychiatrists as well as everybody else.[2]

It is worth remembering that a fairly high percentage of the people in every church who become known as trouble-makers are people who feel they are slipping—either in their vocations or in their status at church—and they find it hard to adjust to the situation.

In contrast to this, however, we sometimes find it hard to love our fellow Christians more because of their virtues than because "the old Adam" is resurrected in them. Who are harder to reconcile than a group of people with differing convictions, all held with religious passion? Speaking of the men working under his direction, one mission superintendent confessed that "the hardest part of being a Superintendent is learning to live with so many diverse consciences among the brethren!"

All of this is to say that the church, like the world, is full of people with problems. Their problems differ widely both in their nature and their intensity, and the individuals who make up the congregation vary in their ability to find constructive solutions. But problems they all have.

If you knew the inner secrets of the people who make up the average congregation, you would know that in addition to the large number who are mature and faithful followers of Christ, there are also those who are without faith, conscience, or emotional stability. There are unhappily married couples struggling to maintain the appearance of respectability, lonely people flirting with suicide, heartless people dreaming of murder, dishonest people scheming treachery, disillusioned people shedding all evidence of faith but the outward show of it, and bitter people compulsively pushing concepts of hate under the banner of Christian love.

These are the people the churchman must love. This implies more than is involved in the overplayed concept

[2] *The Status Seekers* (New York: David McKay Company, Inc., 1959), p. 256.

of "the friendly church." Believe me, church people should be friendly, and a "cold church" is a contradiction in terms. Yet, nothing about a church is said more or means less than that it is friendly. So is your Shell dealer. This truth struck me with a sudden impact once when my wife and I attended Sunday worship in a church where we were visitors. As we entered the narthex, we were ambushed by greeters who emerged from the cloistered shadows to which our sun-strained eyes were not yet adjusted. At the insistence of one, I was lured off to the right to sign our names in the guest book while my wife was whisked to the left for the same purpose. After a few innocuous questions about who we were and where we were from and were we vacationing and wasn't that nice, we were finally reunited and ushered through the door past a couple of men who were gracious enough to say nothing, but to hand us our printed orders of service. It was the kind of gauntlet I don't enjoy running. Those greeters had nothing to say to me at that time and place, nor I to them. If their purpose was to prove that their church was friendly, I suppose they succeeded, although I didn't need the proof. Their worship sheet contained a cordial invitation to the coffee hour following the service and, had I been looking for someone to talk with, I should have accepted. It was at the coffee hour that the greeters should have been most active rather than at the vestibule to the sanctuary.

I am sure that many disagree with my attitude about this. Even my wife, a very mature person and one to whom worship means as much as it does to me, finds no offense in these aggressive preservice greetings. There must be others, however, who feel much the same as I. Probably they are the ones church-membership committees hold meetings about to ask why they have stopped coming. And the answer, if anyone ever gets it, will be "superficiality."

More than a commercialized brand of friendly treatment for all is needed. Human life runs deep. Intelligent people know this, and turn to the church, hoping to find others who know it too. No friendly greeter reciting stock questions and looking beyond you to the next arrival mounting the stairs, gives much promise. Neither does the minister who, in spite of bold announcements that he is available for counseling any time of day or night, can't talk with you thirty minutes without getting nervous about his next deadline. But it doesn't matter. If he is that busy he isn't operating at your depth anyway. With so little time for prayer and study, his own little spring of living water must be close to running dry.

One day I received a letter from a young woman who was asking the kinds of questions one doesn't put to a greeter in the narthex or to a minister on his way to a board meeting. I am going to quote from it at some length because it contains the stuff from which true Christian fellowship emerges. After a brief preliminary paragraph, she launched directly into what meant most to her:

> I know you believe in God, and I suppose I must say that I believe in God, too. God must be the ultimate reality, whatever that is . . . Would you attribute to this God personal characteristics, such as intelligence, concern for the individual, love? If you would do this, do you feel that there is the possibility of communication between Him (or It) and people? If so, what is the nature of this communication? Does prayer have any other function than meditative reorganization of our own thinking which we could do as well in another form? Or does it serve as a way of satisfying our desire for security, reassurance, and personal importance? Is there an ultimate reality other than what we concoct in our minds to satisfy our needs and desires and to fill in the holes in our knowledge and understanding that cannot be filled by other means at our disposal?

She continues:

> Now it seems possible to me that one could go on living quite a while without answers to these ques-

tions. However, it would be very difficult to live in any reasonable fashion without some kind of ethical or moral idea after which to pattern one's behavior.

Expressing doubt as to what the basis of one's behavior should be she says:

> I am not willing to accept the dictates of society merely because they are dictated by society, nor the morality of Christianity merely because it is propounded in the Bible, nor the ideas of my parents merely because they have been taught me since before I can remember.

And she asks:

> What criteria are safe and valid?
>
> Do you think the world, or the universe, or ultimate reality is good or bad or neutral?
>
> Do you think people are supposed to be happy, or does real living come only through suffering?
>
> Do you think there is survival of human personality after death other than through our influence on other people?
>
> Do you think it's possible to be unselfish, *really*?
>
> What is spiritual love?
>
> What is emotional maturity, and how can it be achieved?

You might conclude that anyone with that many problems is in need of some counseling. Probably so. We all are. And the church is the place to get it. It is a kind of spiritual therapy center where persons with problems can come and be frank about their problems without fear of censure. Here people learn to accept one another just as they are, and in the process learn to accept themselves. The spirit of it is caught in a gospel hymn we used to sing. How modern is its psychology!

> Just as I am, without one plea,
> . . .
> Just as I am, and waiting not
> To rid my soul of one dark blot.
> . . .
> Just as I am, though tossed about
> With many a conflict, many a doubt,
> Fightings and fears within, without,
> . . .

Because the church, ideally, accepts people as they are, it is in a position to help them. It points out that Christ also accepts them as they are, and his love redeems them. That's what the song is about:

> Just as I am! Thou wilt receive,
> Wilt welcome, pardon, cleanse, relieve;
> . . .
> Just as I am! Thy love unknown
> Hath broken every barrier down;
> Now, to be Thine, yea, Thine alone,
> O Lamb of God I come!

That's what happens in that fellowship that is the church. People are accepted as they are. Barriers fall, and life is renewed.

Whatever else you may say about it, the church, like the Sabbath, is for people. It is a fellowship into which they may bring their sins, their immaturities, their jealousies, their angers, their hatreds, their misunderstandings, as well as their love and goodwill. It is important for laymen to understand this if they are to learn what it means to know and to love the members of the church.

The traditional services the church offers its members are involved here. Genuinely concerned for one another, laymen will call on the sick and shut-ins to bring them the healing ministry of Christ. They will listen sympathetically to one another's problems, and pitch in to help when trouble comes. The old idea that these are functions to be confined to ordained clergy will pass away, and the church fellowship will grow rich with shared affection as all join in the ministry of pastoral concern.

VIII

The Enemy in the Pew

The church is at war and Christianity is engaged in a battle. There is nothing new or startling about this. Jesus said he came to bring a sword and to set his followers at odds with the people around them. Paul spoke of being armed for the fight, and many of our hymns—sung to martial tunes—are battle hymns.

Who is the church's adversary? Some say the Devil. But they have a hard time drawing a bead on him and the suspicion persists that he is a phantom. Others focus on whatever world power is currently playing the Goliath role and seek to equate the Christian's battle with national defense. Still others say the enemy is anger, lust, sloth, and the other four of the seven "deadly sins."

No doubt there is truth in all of these assertions, but I want to suggest that the enemy is no one person or nation. The enemy is a spirit, an attitude, a manner of thinking. And he may be found in the church pew. The disciples had their Judas and families have their black sheep. Church families are no exception. Whatever evil there may be outside the church, there are always enemies within.

Take for example the spirit of status seeking. Both individually as Christians and unitedly as Christian institutions, we have become addicted to luxury and dedicated to the pursuit of status in this American economy of abundance.

Indeed, the churches themselves are infected with the success bug. A new building gives us status; large crowds bespeak popularity. We covet praise and consider it a special honor if someone of notoriety attends our service and compliments us, even if that person is religiously illiterate and morally corrupt. Both as individuals and as churches we are eager to be successful in the eyes of the world.

Jesus was very hard on that kind of spirit. The Scribes and Pharisees were near the top of the success ladder, and Jesus told people not to be like them for they had grown corrupt in the society that had favored them. He cautioned his followers about too much popularity. "Woe to you, when all men speak well of you," he said (Luke 6:26). He suggested that the right way to live is to take your place at the foot of the table and be the servant—scarcely attractive advice to the young man on his way up. At least one man didn't like it. He was really a model of success: rich, powerful, attractive, and virtuous besides. A man of tact, he was careful not to upset anybody. "Master," he began, "I know that you are good . . ." (Phillips). He started with a compliment, and he did it without ever having taken a Dale Carnegie course. He knew this was a good way to fend off criticism. No one is likely to attack a person who has just praised him. No doubt he expected Jesus to return the compliment and say something nice about him. Then they could have a pleasant talk, and he could depart to report to his friends, "I like the new preacher. He's a good fellow, just like the rest of us." But Jesus didn't respond the way he was supposed to. He talked like a psychiatrist. He examined the motive behind the young man's compliment. "I wonder why you call me good?" he asked (Phillips). Up to that point this man of wealth and position had been able to hold his world steady by being nice to people, but this impertinent fellow stuck his crowbar under the compliment and flipped it over, exposing the ugly, creeping motives beneath it.

Jesus was a man with a battle to fight and he was tracking down the enemy—the questionable motive hiding behind the camouflage of compliment. "We must clean the enemy out of here," he was saying. "You must change."

No doubt it was unnerving to this "young man of the year" to have his sales pitch upset and to be told that maybe what was needed in the world was for men like him to change. But change is exactly what the man of "status" can't assimilate. That's why any controversial figure frightens him so and any forward thrust of society is considered a mark of instability. People who think they are already successful have little incentive for innovations. At the top of the heap, they sit hard on the society that has elevated them to their lofty position. They are determined to hold it steady, but they will never succeed.

Roughly speaking, there are three competing forces in all human societies. One is *the force of violent change*. Never far below the surface, it is explosive in nature and expresses itself in riots and revolutions. The second is *the force opposing all change*. This tends to be represented by the elite of any society, the "successful" men who have everything to gain and nothing to lose by keeping things as they are. The third is *the force working for peaceful change*.

The third force characterizes the church at its best, and sets it forever at odds with those elements within society which seek either to rise to the top by blowing everything up, or to stay at the top by holding everything down. This puts the church in a very difficult position, for it is always in danger of being captured by one extreme or the other. But the church must never sell out to either group. It opposes the violent revolutionary on the one hand, saying,

"You can't build a great society by blowing it up," and it opposes the reactionary on the other, warning, "You can make no permanent gains for yourself by holding the other fellow down."

When James Kidd, a Scottish preacher, was moving from the old manse where he and his family had lived so long, he found it very difficult to leave. Even after the furniture had been taken out, he lingered on, walking through the empty rooms, noting the bedroom where the children were born and the study where he had prepared his sermons and prayed through many a knotty problem and the parlor where he had talked with his church people through long hours. But suddenly his reverie was broken when Betty, their servant girl, pleaded, "Come away sir, come away. The time's up, and the other house is far better than this!"

Those of us who have worked hard to achieve certain things for ourselves and our society, and have won a degree of success, are understandably inclined to linger on with things as they are. But we must understand that any success achieved is no success at all, but only a platform from which to launch another advance. Again and again we must respond to the servant girl's plea: "Come away sir, come away." The time is up for narrow nationalism, and the other house is far better than this. The time is up for unrestricted militarism, and the other house is far better than this. The time is up for segregation, and the other house is far better than this. The church is at war, and the enemy is the spirit of status-seeking and advantage-holding that is found in all of us.

A second enemy among us is the spirit of self-righteousness. It is the moralistic attitude which seems to say, "The world is in a terrible mess: 'The Catholics want to run America.' 'There is too much drinking.' 'You can't trust the Communists.' 'The sex standards among young people are shocking.' 'Those Negroes are pushing too fast.'" These accusations may be true or false. My own conviction is that some are accurate and some are not. But the point is this: When the moralist making these accusations is a Protestant churchman who never took a drink in his life, never knowingly came face to face with a Communist, has long since passed his youth and is agreeably if not happily married, and is securely ensconced in an upper-middle-class white neighborhood, his accusations have little significance. He is not fighting the Christian battle. He isn't even on the battlefield.

The young man Jesus talked with was somewhat like that. To be sure, he came to ask Jesus how he could be better, but it wasn't because he thought he was particularly sinful. On the contrary, he saw himself as a model of circumspect behavior. Look at the confidence, not to say egotism, present in the glib claim that he had kept all of the commandments since he was quite young. Oh? Had he never born false witness, never said anything about another that wasn't quite true? Had he never coveted the possessions of another? Surely a man could not reach his position of affluence without now and then casting an envious glance at someone who possessed something he didn't have. There is not much doubt about it: this young man figured he lived the good life, and if there were anything wrong about him, it couldn't amount to much. Sin was something he associated almost exclusively with other people, so it was their problem, not his.

Back in my seminary days, I was once asked to preach in the school chapel. Afterwards a group of students, along with Dr. Edwin Booth, our professor of church history, went to lunch together. As we sat around someone asked Dr. Booth what he thought of the sermon. He said, "What I can't understand is why a man who can preach like that can't get better grades in church history." I figured that was his problem. He was the one who gave out the grades.

See how easy it is to slip out from under responsibility for our own shortcomings and point the finger of blame at the other fellow? We all have the tendency to locate the enemy outside ourselves and to withdraw from the battlefield. If we can just be convinced that the real culprit is the NAACP, or the White Citizens' Council, or the Communists, or the Birchers, a tremendous load is lifted from our own consciences and we can go on with the comfortable illusion that we have kept the commandments since our youth.

In this country where even the humblest among us have a strong temptation to consider ourselves superior to others, if for no other reason than that we are Americans, self-righteousness is a plague. We are prone to boast of this land of ours as though we were personally responsible for its greatness. One writer, addressing himself to the question of what national purpose we have beyond securing the benefits of an affluent society for ourselves, came to the conclusion that our goal is "to confer upon the inhabitants of the whole earth the benefits of our own prosperity and our own way of life." But Joseph Wood Krutch asks penetratingly: "Are we so sure that we Americans lead not only a good life, but the very best life, and that an adequate national purpose is simply to spread it far and wide?" The very fact that we would assume this to be the case is evidence of our self-righteousness.

It shows up in church where the self-righteous worshiper is willing to support missionaries to help the unfortunates who didn't have the good sense to be born in this country. He will even pray for them, but assuming that if God thought highly of them He would have endowed them with the good fortune he himself enjoys, he doesn't do it with much optimism. Indeed, he has so little faith in the power of the gospel, once planted, to work as a leaven in a country, he resents the missionary money that was poured into China through the years, and half suspects that much of what he now gives will be similarly "wasted." In his self-righteousness he is suspicious and critical of what happens in any "foreign" land.

There is a need for churchmen to confess their own sins.

Alcoholics Anonymous has learned the importance of this. Testimonies at AA meetings characteristically begin with the preface, "I am an alcoholic." This is done even when the speaker hasn't had a drink for years. He knows his essential nature and he knows that without his constant vigilance alcohol could get the better of him again. Similarly, we Christians in pew and pulpit should admit without hesitation, "I am self-righteous," knowing that this is a battle that has to be won over again every couple of hours. The church is at war, and one enemy is the self-righteousness in all of us.

This brings us to the third enemy in the pew: irrelevancy. It was in the man Jesus confronted. Jesus said to him, "There is still one thing you have missed. Sell everything you have and give the money away to the poor" (Phillips). Or, in other words, get yourself deeply involved in the world about you. This price was too great to pay and the record says the young man went away in sorrow. He had a beautiful religion but he just couldn't bring himself to apply it to his world.

One day a patient began her hour with her psychiatrist by saying, "Before I begin talking today, Doctor, I want to say something." Many a churchman talks without saying anything. He speaks out, but misses the point. He gives answers to questions no one is asking. The only solutions he has are for the unimportant problems, and the causes to which he dedicates himself, often with fervor, are those that have already been lost or won. He may enter the fight, but on the wrong battlefield; he may shoot his gun, but at the wrong target. He lives in a dream world and is out of touch with what is really going on.

For some reason or other, religious people seem especially prone to close their eyes to the real issues and give their attention to nonessentials. At least a good many of the most competent observers of the human scene are telling us that. Norman Cousins, in his book *In Place of Folly,* says that one of the enemies of society is "any man in the pulpit who is . . . a dispenser of balm rather than an awakener of conscience" and who is preoccupied with helping people find personal peace of mind instead of creating "a blazing sense of restlessness to set things right." And one theological professor confesses: "It is so easy for Christianity to become so polite, so respectable, so neat, so conventional—and so sterile and irrelevant." One man put us in our place when he said, "For most of us religion has become one of the twenty-five departments in *Time Magazine*." He says, hopelessly, "We have nothing to say to the world, and the world knows it." Then with a final thrust he adds that in America, religion "has become a very general and vacuous business, more concerned about supporting 'a way of life in the American style' than in obedience to Jesus Christ."

That's a serious indictment, but there is truth in it. It is a very great temptation for Protestant Christians to think of their church as a safe harbor, protecting them from the wild storms of a turbulent society instead of a seaworthy ship to plow into the teeth of the storm.

Most of us as modern American Protestants are afraid to get involved. We continue to nourish the illusion that we are untainted. Taking a safe position above the sociopolitical ferment, we find it a good deal more comfortable to maintain the fiction that we are nice people, practicing the true religion that will someday be predominant in the world, than to run the risk of causing dissension in our own ranks by muddying our feet in controversial matters. The artificial world we have built up seems much safer than the real world, and in the familiar environment of hymns and prayers, we find it easier to believe that we are "God's chosen people." Sheltered in our sanctuaries we don't have to face the frightening truth that in some large metropolitan centers where the races of mankind battle poverty and prejudice, we are known as WASPS: white Anglo-Saxon Protestants!

But there are signs of renewal in the church. There is growing evidence that the church is relevant to society after all. One Sunday I worshiped in a little Methodist Church on the edge of the French Quarter in New Orleans. The archway over the front entrance is blackened by creosote bombs that were thrown at the church in angry protest against the minister, Andy Foreman, who walked daily through a screaming mob to take his little girl to an integrated school.

Sometime later a bomb exploded in a Negro church in Birmingham, killing four children and injuring others. The whole nation was stunned and the reverberations were felt around the world. People who didn't know a soul in Birmingham felt the hurt of it and wept. Yet the blackened archway of the white Methodist Church in New Orleans and the smoking debris of the Negro Baptist Church in Birmingham, like the cross of Jesus Christ, constitute a great symbol of hope. They represent what the cross always represents, the point at which the love of God encounters the bitter hatred of man. And for Protestant Americans they are visible evidence that the Christian message, channeled through the church can still be relevant to human society.

George MacLeod[1] of the Iona Community in Scotland was in South Africa some time ago and was scheduled to address a large public gathering in Durban. Shortly before the meeting began a prominent citizen approached him saying, "I hope you are going to give them the gospel red hot." "Yes," he answered, "I am speaking of its social implications here in Durban." "Social implications?" he asked, suspiciously. "What is wanted is the gospel red hot." "But," asked MacLeod, "is it not of the gospel that by the right of Christ all men have an equal dignity?" "Yes," he agreed. "That is of the gospel." "Then what are you Gospellers doing about the 10,000 Africaans and Indians who have not got a decent shelter in Durban this cold night?" asked the preacher. And the hot-Gospeller replied, "Them?

[1] *Only One Way Left* (Glasgow, Scotland: The Iona Community House, 1956), p. 54.

I wish the whole damn lot were sunk in the harbour!" And MacLeod says that that man could recite the Christian creeds immaculately and was sure of his own salvation in Christ.

Pleading for Christian involvement in the world, a gospel that is relevant to the lives men actually lead, MacLeod says:

> I simply argue that the Cross be raised again at the centre of the market place as well as on the steeple of the church. I am recovering the claim that Jesus was not crucified in a Cathedral between two candles, but on a Cross between two thieves; on the town garbage heap; on a crossroads so cosmopolitan that they had to write his title in Hebrew and Latin and in Greek (or shall we say in English, in Bantu, and in Afrikaans); at the kind of place where cynics talk smut, and thieves curse, and soldiers gamble. Because that is where He died and that is what He died about. And that is where Churchmen should be and what churchmen should be about.[2]

The church is at war and the enemy is the spirit of irrelevancy among the church's own members. This is a fact that most laymen find very difficult to understand. And while both ministers and laymen are tempted to protect the church from rough encounters with society as a whole, it is the laymen more than it is the ministers who are afraid for the church to get involved. Historian James H. Nichols is convinced of this. He says that "the American Protestant clergy as a group have a far more adequate conception of the implications of the Gospel for the whole community than have the laity . . ." Confirming this opinion, theologian Georgia Harkness has pointed out that the laity have "lagged behind the clergy in their grasp of the implications of the Gospel for the community," and have

[2] *Ibid.*, p. 38.

often "stifled prophetic utterance that might disturb the *status quo.*" In what amounts to a real indictment of the laity she says: "It is in general the laymen rather than the clergy who keep white churches white, who oppose integration in the public schools, who do not want civil rights legislation to be passed in Congress or placed in party platforms." The same is true, she affirms, with regard to matters of economics. The layman can be depended upon to line up with economic conservatism. He tends to equate the free enterprise system with the Kingdom of God and to suspect the disloyalty of any preacher who insists on judging it in terms of the Christian ethic. He responds to generalized appeals for gifts to relieve the oppressed, but he resents any application of the gospel to local or national economic affairs.

Similarly, Dr. Harkness points out, with regard to nationalism, the average layman seems to equate being a good Christian with being a good American. "To many laymen—perhaps to most—there is no clear sense of contrast between the sovereignty of the nation and the sovereignty of God."

The problem seems to be that the typical layman has lost sight of the ultimate Christian principles by which all things are to be judged. He maintains and nourishes a body of emotional reactions to social issues and mistakes these for Christian principles. "Because I feel this strongly," he reasons unconsciously, "it must be Christian." "Because a Negro next door, a radical change in our economic system, or a marked reduction in arms is a frightening thing to think of, and a terrible threat to me, it is, of course unchristian." His conclusions may or may not be right, but his reasons for them are dead wrong. "My opinion," or, more positively, "my conviction" has become his ultimate authority. But his "opinion" or "conviction" just might happen to be off base—even if it corresponds with the majority opinion of his community or nation. Says Dr. Harkness, "It is not the business of the Church, or of any Christian in it, to claim to have all the answers. It is the business of the Church to hold every proposed line of action up to Christian scrutiny—to throw the searchlight of the gospel upon every issue which affects the lives and destinies of persons in God's world. Ministers can do some of this; laymen by their closeness to the issues can do more —and do it more effectively—if they will."[3]

Few, however, have caught the vision. Meanwhile the church continues to do much that is irrelevant to what is going on in the world. This is an enemy to be conquered.

A fourth enemy is ignorance. One cannot be relevant to a society he doesn't understand. It is possible for church people to know a great deal about the so-called "spiritual life" and very little about the hard facts of living. The stained glass they live behind sometimes distorts their vision of the world. Such people are not only blind to the facts, but they are blind to the fact they are blind to the facts. They are like Alexander Pope whose "Essay on Man" was ridiculed by Samuel Johnson. Johnson said that "Pope had read Bollingbrook, and not understanding him was naturally anxious to explain him to others." Those who know the least are often the surest of their knowledge. How confidently they express convictions on social issues, yet how little they know about why they prefer to live in all-white neighborhoods, why they change their ideas about social justice as they climb up the socioeconomic ladder, or what the real issues are between Christianity and Communism.

They are often deluded because of the powerful forces outside themselves that make up their minds for them. They take on the ideas of whatever social unit is really dominant in their lives and state them as their own convictions, often supporting them with Biblical or other authoritative sanction.

The delusion is perhaps most transparent with teenagers. This is because they are less experienced in deceiving them-

[3] *The Church and Its Laity* (New York: Abingdon Press, 1962), pp. 128–133.

selves and others and less subtle about expressing their ideas. So, when your fourteen-year-old daughter insists on wearing bizarre clothing and a porcupine hair-do, chews gum noisily, and flies into a rage because she isn't allowed to come in at whatever hour she chooses, you soon learn that she is simply being a teenager. She is just a mirror, reflecting the standards of the social group with which she wants most to rate at the moment. Yet she thinks the ideas she expresses are her own. She doesn't realize that if suddenly that entire teenage crowd were to melt away, her whole personality would be changed.

But teenagers are not the only ones who are victims of this kind of delusion. All of us are more a product of our social set than we would like to admit. John Galbraith, in *The Affluent Society*, uses a term that describes the situation. He speaks of the "conventional wisdom." By this he means those ideas that are accepted as "kosher" in your group. Thus, if you are going to be on the "in" with liberal Democrats, you must give evidence that you are a "tried and true" liberal, by faithfully adhering to the basic ideas that are "acceptable" with that group. You just wouldn't last long in that setting if you went on a campaign to muzzle the labor unions, reduce government controls, and retreat into pre-1914 isolationism. On the other hand if you have chosen to identify yourself with conservative Republicans you will know just how to recite the creed about creeping socialism, free enterprise, and the dangers of big government. And, unless you are among the fortunate ones who can get outside themselves and see the humor of the situation, you are just as blind as the teenager to the fact that you aren't being a creative individual at all but just a reflection of the group to which you belong.

Take vocational groups, for example. Each has its own "conventional wisdom." When you choose a vocation you are choosing more than the kind of work you expect to do. You are choosing the kind of people you will associate with and the kinds of attitudes you will have about society as a whole, and life in general. For example, a man studying to be a doctor is not just learning the nature of the human body and how to treat it; he is also learning the "correct" way to react to chiropractors and Medicare. Educators are learning, in addition to what and how to teach, just what social attitudes are good for the whole profession. And ministers learn, in addition to some theology, the pious manner in which they must give God the credit for the bishop's mistake in appointing them to the finest church in the area.

Arthur Koestler wrote about a kind of a puzzle he used to play with when he was a child. Its basic unit was a piece of paper with a tangle of red and blue lines on it. Looking at it directly you could make nothing meaningful out of it. But if you put a piece of thin red tissue paper over it, the red lines were blotted out, and the blue lines made a picture of a clown in a circus, holding a hoop for a dog to jump through. If you put transparent blue paper over it, the blue lines disappeared and the red lines revealed a lion chasing a clown around the ring.

It's a good analogy. How we look at the world depends on the color of the tissue paper we see it through. The whole fabric of society looks quite different, depending on whether you are viewing it through the eyes of a Southern Negro janitor, a wealthy widow who has never been near poverty, a moving-picture actress who has risen from a lower-middle-class childhood to stardom, or a top-flight business executive. Each will see the country and the world in terms of the society that most closely surrounds him. Such a limited view constitutes ignorance.

This simple-mindedness is interestingly illustrated in the experience of Elisabeth Elliot, widow of one of the five missionaries murdered by the Auca Indians. As she began to lay plans to reach the Aucas with the Christian message, and thus accomplish what her husband and the other men had failed to do, she received a shower of advice from people all over the world. One person sent her sixty dollars to buy Bibles for the Aucas who, of course, have no written language and who know no language other than their own. Another woman suggested that the Ten Commandments be written on a slip of paper and dropped to the Aucas from an airplane. Says Elisabeth Elliot, "Suggestions gleaned from encyclopedias, seances, Greek mythology, and Freudian psychology poured in." That illustrates our point exactly. Each person viewing the problem from his particular setting had his neat, but usually very inadequate, solution.

This is what is going on in today's world. The average American, with his smattering of newspaper knowledge of world affairs presumes himself to be competent to express convictions. The result is that gigantic global problems are dreadfully oversimplified as each person views them from his little corner. And nine times out of ten what he sees from his little corner is more or less unimportant, and almost certainly biased.

This lays a tremendous responsibility at the door of the church. Christian laymen must set high standards of involvement in world issues. They must open their eyes and take a new look at the church, the world, human nature, Christianity, and every proposed solution to today's problems. They must develop a new awareness of social issues, and they must gain a clearer insight into the subtle pressures that force them into group, rather than independent, judgments concerning those issues.

Peter Berger, perceptive sociologist, portrays our plight convincingly in his picture of a puppet theater in which the characters are "running about to and fro on the stage, going through the motions of the play—all the time with keys turning slowly and perceptibly in their backs." He says our human society is like that, but with one decisive difference: "We may, indeed, be puppets of society, but with a strange, almost sinister capacity. For we can stop in our tracks, turn around and look over our shoulders—and perceive the keys turning in our backs. This act of consciousness is the first step into freedom."

The Christian layman should work hard to make the church the center of just this kind of consciousness (truth) that makes us free. He, of all people, should be quick to recognize self-deception, and rise above it.

One of the most magnificent transformations that Jesus Christ effects in us is that he unmasks us. He is the enemy of sham. If there is one thing he never could endure it is pretense. He condemned the Scribes and Pharisees because they were "play-actors." He called them "blind leaders," and again, more descriptively, "blind idiots." "Have you no eyes?" he asked. He called them "utter frauds" and said they called themselves leaders but couldn't "see an inch before (their) noses." They were so lacking in perception, he maintained that they would "filter out a mosquito and swallow a camel." Listen to him: "What miserable frauds you are . . . Can't you see? . . . You are a mass of pretence" (brief quotes, Phillips). Nothing, it would appear to me, aroused his anger like the blindness of "good" people. And he was forever counseling his followers to know the truth, for it leads to freedom.

For the ignorance of those who had never had a real chance to be enlightened—like the illiterate of our day—he had great pity. Perhaps it was of such persons he was speaking when he said, "Father forgive them; for they know not what they do" (Luke 23:34). A genuine lack of knowledge is to be forgiven. But such tenderness seems to have been withheld from the Scribes and Pharisees who were ignorant in the midst of knowledge. He would understand the cartoon picturing a crucifix superimposed on a mushroom cloud, and carrying the caption, "Forgive them not. They know what they do." In any event, the Christian layman should know what is going on in the world; he should understand the Christian faith; and he should know how the one relates to the other. Ignorance in the pew is an enemy.

Another enemy in the pew is fear. We are afraid of revealing our weaknesses, so we never deal with them adequately. We are afraid of making a mistake, so we withdraw from the venture that should have claimed us. We are afraid of criticism, so we silence the conviction that needs to be spoken.

One day a woman wrote a little ditty called "The 101 Percenter" and sent it to a newspaper columnist. It was a simple little thing that read like this:

> When some bellow
> "Patriotic!"
> It sounds more like
> "Hate-riotic!"

Shortly after this was in the mail, she sent a second letter to the journalist, special delivery, saying, "After I mailed my two-liner I mentioned it to my husband and he said he hoped I hadn't used my own name as we might get bombed or at least some obnoxious phone calls. Therefore, if you print it, would you use the initials G.F.?" And the columnist stated simply, "A sad state of affairs."

Sad indeed. And sadder because it is no isolated incident. A brilliant student in a Southern California high school, preparing a term paper on Russia, wrote to the Russian embassy for some material. But she wrote under an assumed name to make sure no one linked her with the "enemy." The teacher who told me that story said that he could understand her action because he had sometimes been tempted to do the same kind of thing. Again, "a sad state of affairs."

If we are to be relevant to the facts of our time then we must step on our fears and face reality. If Jesus had no use for pretense, he had no use for cowardice either. Along with his appeals to face the truth were his constant reminders to have no fear.

Now let me mention another enemy to be found in the pew: helplessness. This is the little fellow who, in the face of world revolutions, retreats into inactivity.

Speaking of this kind of person, Norman Cousins says: "His main article of faith is that there are mammoth forces at work which the individual cannot possibly comprehend, much less alter or direct." If he is a private citizen, this man "delegates his worries about the world to officialdom. He assumes that only the people in authority are in a position to know and act. On the other hand, if he is a public official himself, he declares his helplessness to do anything without a mandate from the people." In either situation he satisfies his conscience that, when it comes to world problems, there is nothing he needs to do.

This man is the enemy in the pew because he has the power to prevent disaster and isn't using it. He is the enemy because his lethargy leaves the field to extremists of right and left who aren't timid about proposing answers to world problems, but who have bad answers. He is the enemy because, as Jesus said, "He who is not with me is against me" (Matt. 12:30).

James Wechsler, editor and columnist of the *New York Post*, says that too many of us think "we can do nothing more than sit around, keep our fists up and try to concentrate on the comforts of life." William J. Lederer suggests that we have become a people who let someone else worry about the big problems while we promote our private enterprises. Convinced that we can do nothing about the great world issues anyway, we just take the report of our favorite news journal at face value, cluck over how dreadful it all is, and return to our bridge game. In this same vein, Karl Menninger, speaking from the viewpoint of psychiatry, says that "most Americans today exist without purpose and without significance. They have no articulate philosophy; they do not live within any frame of reference."

Meanwhile, men in other parts of the globe have called attention to the same problem. The late Prime Minister Nehru once said, "This is a dangerous world in which we live, and complacency on our part will be ruinous." Norman MacKenzie has declared that in Britain, men of ideals have "talked themselves into a mood of resignation and retreated into private worlds." Surely Yeats was describing our time even more accurately than his own when he wrote:

> The best lack all conviction, while the worst
> Are full of passionate intensity.

However you phrase it, the simple fact is that the world is falling apart, and a large percentage of its Christian citizens seem content to let it tumble.

These people may be grouped in different categories. Some of them are simply *unrelated* to what is going on in the world. They are quite unaware that anything momentous is happening. All their lives they have heard about strange people in faraway places doing outrageous things, but this didn't particularly affect them. And they see today's headlines in about the same light. It's like reading a novel. The story concerns people who never really existed. It's interesting to read about them, but you can't be expected to jump between the covers of the book and solve their problems for them. For these people, world affairs are something to read about, not something to participate in. Content with the confidence that America is a giddy success and we have nothing to worry about except that someone might want to take it away from us (and even that isn't much of a worry since we could hurt them worse than they could hurt us), they go back and forth to their daily work and attend church on Sunday as if there were necessarily something permanent about their way of life.

Another group of helpless people we may call the *preoccupied*. Inwardly disturbed, they are too much involved with their personal problems to be capable of relating to the world outside of them. They can't do anything about a shattered world until they find some unity in their own lives. In extreme form these are the psychotics who are simply out of touch with reality.

A third group of helpless people may be identified as the *indolent*—an ugly word. It means mostly lazy, but it applies to a lot of laymen. These people know we are in trouble, so they can't plead ignorance; and they have personal resources they could throw into the fight, so they can't plead inability. But they just don't act. They are as irresponsible as the man who was reported as playing golf on the Bel-Air Golf Course when refugees from the dreadful Bel-Air fire gathered near the green where he was playing to watch their homes go up in flames. "Woman," he screamed at one of the ladies, "stop sobbing while I'm putting."

An early scene in Reynolds Price's novel, *A Long and Happy Life*, shows Rosacoke, a girl about twenty years old, at the funeral of Mildred, a Negro girl whom she had known since childhood. Mildred had died in giving birth to an illegitimate child. As the funeral in the old country church proceeds, the preacher calls on the white girl to "testify" in behalf of her friend. "If you could find anything in your heart to say," says the preacher, "we would be mighty glad." She couldn't think of much, but she stood up and said, "I hadn't seen much of Mildred lately, but we always observed each other's birthday, her and me, and the other evening I thought to myself, it is nearly Mildred's twenty-first birthday so I walked down to her place after supper, and nobody was there except the turkey. I didn't know till the next afternoon they had carried her away. There I was just wanting to give her a pair of stockings and wish her a long and happy life and she was already gone."

That's about the way many laymen appear before the world today. They feel a certain kinship to "the other half" even if they don't like the turkeys in their yards, and they like to take them a little something now and then. Suddenly they find themselves standing there with a couple of CARE packages in their hands, just wanting to wish them a long and happy life. It seems the least a Christian can do. But they are quite unmindful of the tragic circumstances that engulf them and in the face of which a casual gesture of benevolence is almost an insult. They might have done something really constructive if they hadn't been so helpless.

Here, then, are some of the enemies to be found in the pew: status seeking, self-righteousness, irrelevancy, ignorance, fear, and helplessness. How can we ever conquer them? There is just one way: To rediscover the true nature of the Christian faith and be loyal to it. We must somehow deepen the dedication of church members until their lives are plainly given over to one purpose only, complete obedience to God's will as it is revealed to them.

Obedience has come to be an ugly word in our time. We took it out of the marriage ceremony, and we are reluctant to apply it even to children except when they are very small. It is too authoritarian to find a comfortable place in our climate of permissiveness. To obey another, we have come to feel, is an outrage against our selfhood, crippling our creativity and offending our freedom of self-expression.

The idea of compulsion is highly objectionable to us. We have no desire to take orders from anybody. We prefer to sit down and talk things over. Thus in business we bargain with one another. In the professions we consult and counsel. In school we share. Our newspapers carry letters to the editor. Our churches offer endless opportunities to serve on committees or participate in discussion groups, and in our homes we have our family councils. That, we say, is what democracy is all about.

But we are wrong when we suppose that the Kingdom of God is a democracy, that the Christian faith is a constitution that can be changed by popular vote or that God is a presiding officer, open-minded and willing to be convinced. God is a King who rules by divine right. His laws are inexorable. He is not to be bargained with but obeyed. As Paul puts its, it is not mere knowledge of the will of God that is important, but *obedience* to it. In his famous defense before King Agrippa he tells how his vision of Christ is the inspiration of his life and declares, "I could not *disobey* the heavenly vision" (Phillips). In his letters he repeatedly calls upon the Christians to be obedient to the faith, reminding them that even Jesus "humbled himself by living a life of utter *obedience* . . ." (Phillips). With every nerve in his body crying out against God's orders that night in Gethsemane, Christ *obeyed* God's will and pushed his own aside.

I suspect that there is nothing in Christianity more important but less understood than that the Christian faith demands obedience. We tell our young people to get the facts and decide for themselves. We should tell them to listen for the voice of God speaking through the facts, and obey!

Contradictory as it may sound, freedom is found in obedience. This is illustrated in the most famous words of Martin Luther. "Here stand I," he declared, in a bold affirmation of personal freedom that has challenged independent thinkers ever since. But don't forget the rest of his statement: "God help me; I can do no other." He was under a divine compulsion to obey. In obedience to God he found the courage to renounce the tyranny of man, and was free.

One of the greatest persons I have been privileged to know, although ever so briefly, was Dr. Paul Harrison. He was a medical missionary in Arabia from the time he finished his medical training until a few years ago when he was forced to retire because of age. He went to Arabia because he wanted to go where he was needed most, and a missionary friend had told him that Arabia was the place with "the worst climate, the most difficult language, the neediest people, and . . . the least chance for success" of any place in the world. Through all of his professional life he did his work under unbelievably difficult circumstances, working with inadequate equipment, poorly trained assistants, and in makeshift operating rooms. Often he was forced to battle not only disease but also prejudice and open hostility in his efforts to bring medical assistance and the Christian faith to people badly in need of both. Yet, remote from the great medical centers, and forced to give his attention to many things besides medicine, he kept himself so well informed of medical advancement that when he retired and returned to the United States, he was able to pass the Florida State medical board examinations and practice medicine in this country. In my brief associations with him I was impressed with his quick mind, his keen sense of humor, his wide range of knowledge, his youthful attitude, his dedication to the Christian faith, and the fact that when he visited our church he insisted on attending both services so he could hear the sermon twice. There was a great man! Unencumbered by prejudices and parochialisms, he was not the captive of any organized medical group, political party, or theological fad. And he seemed to struggle with no personal inhibitions or anxieties. There was the breath of freedom about him. He had the curiosity of a child and the wisdom of an elder statesman. He was a man free to be his true self.

But there was a reason. Years before, when he was a youth, he promised God that he would be a missionary and he could not disobey the heavenly vision. A brilliant student, he went to medical school to prepare himself. He made such an unusual record that near the end of his formal training Dr. Harvey Cushing, head of the department of surgery at Harvard's Peter Bent Brigham Hospital, wrote to him inviting him to join his staff. The invitation to continue medical research with this brilliant surgeon made his head spin with excitement. "You have it in you to go to the top," the famous doctor had written. But the flattery of the invitation did not sway him from his purpose. "Dear Dr. Cushing," he penned with a steady hand, "I thank you for the great honor you have done me in inviting me to work under you. There is nothing I should like to do more *if I were free*. But years ago I determined to use my medical knowledge, such as it is, on a mission field. That is still my purpose." He knew that the Christian faith demands obedience.

Obedient followers of Jesus Christ will ultimately conquer every enemy in pulpit or pew.

IX

Your Part in the Organization

Problems and problem people are best handled within the organized framework of the family. We have said that the church is a family. It is also an organization. We must never forget that. While our minds spin theories and coin phrases about "the gathered church and the dispersed church," "the historical role of the church," and "the theological significance" of it, our feet meander through the mundane mud of institutionalism. Whatever else is to be said about the church, the organizational realities of it are inescapable. The church as we know it is an institution with all of the sins and battle scars appertaining thereto.

And that is a good thing. Institutions are no more evil than skeletons are. Both have the job of holding life together and keeping it upright so that it can go somewhere. To be sure, both are subject to arthritic rigidity and cancerous deterioration. But these conditions are no basis for damning the structure itself. The sins of institutionalism are many and should be corrected, but institutions, even *big* institutions, are not evil *per se*. They are a necessary part of human society and can be abandoned only at subhuman levels.

So let the laymen thank God for the institution of the church, and cooperate with man in perpetuating and strengthening it.

This takes some doing. Churchmanship does not necessarily accompany membership. One does not become a good member of the organization by joining it any more than he becomes a good husband by getting married. To be a good husband a man must assume responsibility for a home. He must learn to pay light bills, adjust to the ways of a woman, care for sick children, maintain good relations with the neighbors, and subordinate his personal needs to the welfare of all without losing the glorious glow of his wedding day. To be a good churchman he must do essentially the same: attend to the daily responsibilities of the church family without losing his sense of joy in being a part of it.

Every church member should accept some specific and appropriate responsibility for the church as an institution just as each member of a family should share in the work required to keep a family going. One of my early memories is the voice of my mother, saying with gentle firmness, "Boys, it's time to do your chores." There was no use debating it. Off we went to burn the trash, feed the rabbits and chickens, milk the goats, and gather the eggs. I cannot imagine that we always went to our work happily, but I do not remember resenting it. Recalling it is pleasant, and I confess to a bit of nostalgia as I think of dipping a container into a "gunny sack" of bran or oats at feeding time, or alternating turns with my brother in milking a goat and holding her hind legs steady to keep a dirty hoof from plunging into the milk bucket. I think the necessity of performing these tasks at specified times each day, along with the feeling that these jobs were specifically ours, gave us satisfaction in the work and an awareness of contributing something of importance to the life of the entire family.

Life in the church family is no different. Acceptance of responsibility for specific areas of its work is a prerequisite to satisfaction within it. Everyone knows the fallacy of raising children in a home where they are given every advantage but no responsibility. The pathetic whimper, "I can't understand it; we never denied him anything," so often heard from parents whose children have no respect for them or the law, is a familiar sound effect in a tragic drama. However, we have been slow to see the similarity between this distortion of family life and the kind of thing that is happening in our churches. Many laymen of all ages must be put in the category of spoiled children. Expecting the church to roll out the white carpet for their wedding ceremonies, be solicitous of them when they have the sniffles, talk them out of their self-induced anxieties, wrap a protective environment of wholesomeness about their youth, and give them the blessing of God Almighty, Father, Son, and Holy Spirit, they sense no duty, on their part, to stand by their church through a long hot summer, or to defend it against its critics. On the contrary, like ungrateful delinquents condemning their parents, they may add to the problems of the church by throwing a few stones of their own. In a show of nonchalance or a pose of injured feelings, they may walk out on it altogether. The fault is our own. We have been too eager to please the members of the church family and too reluctant to assign them their chores. It is the old story of spoiled children.

Fortunately, this error is being recognized, and more and more churches are seeing the need to put the laymen to work if the church's mission is to be fulfilled. There is a saying among psychiatrists that "correct practice brings correct consciousness." If this is true, we are approaching a better understanding of the church, as more and more laymen assume a share of responsibility for its central ministry.

In my denomination, the membership vow involves a

promise to uphold the church "by your prayers, your presence, your gifts, and your service." The first three of these are quite definite and would apply in much the same way to all members. Surely a basic minimum participation for anyone who is at all serious about his churchmanship is to pray for his church daily, attend Sunday worship regularly, and give as generously as he is able.

Daily prayer and weekly church attendance are specific and apply equally to all who are physically and mentally able. When we come to the matter of giving, however, the requirement is less clear-cut. Paul's advice to the Corinthians is a useful guide: "He who sows sparingly will also reap sparingly, and he who sows bountifully will also reap bountifully. Each one must do as he has made up his mind, not reluctantly or under compulsion, for God loves a cheerful giver" (II Cor. 9:6–7).

For the person who wants something more exact to go by, there is no substitute for the tithe. It has the advantage of being both Biblically based and widely accepted today. However, it should be thought of as a minimum standard, within the capacity of all. Many loyal churchmen increase the percentage of their income designated for church purposes as their income grows. Some reach the point where they are able to live on the tenth and give nine-tenths for advancing Christ's work in the world.

Meanwhile, people on limited incomes who want to contribute their tithe are often troubled by a number of theoretical questions about how to determine it. Sometimes the questions are nothing but efforts to rationalize oneself into giving less and enjoying it more. At other times they reflect the painful struggle of exceedingly conscientious people to spread a meager income over all of their family, church, and community responsibilities. Since one never has full knowledge of motivation, I choose to take the questions seriously and to answer them:

1. Should one figure his tithe before taxes or after taxes? Some do it one way and some the other. Take your choice.

2. Should the entire amount of the tithe be given to the church or should some be retained for other benevolent purposes? Here again, conscientious Christians differ in their practices. Some give the entire amount of their tithe to the church and support other benevolences in addition to it. One's relative affluence might have some bearing on this. I should prefer to see people give the total tenth to the church so as not to confuse God's work through his church with other good, but not specifically Christian enterprises. However, either practice prayerfully arrived at and conscientiously followed should leave the churchman with a relatively clear conscience on the matter.

3. If one has a disabled relative he is obligated to support, is this a legitimate claim on his tithe? He will have to decide this for himself and specific circumstances might make a difference. So far as I am concerned, such a matter is a part of my family obligation, not my church obligation.

4. If a person feels he cannot afford a full tithe, can he offer his services as a substitute? This is scarcely possible since service stands on its own as a separate obligation to the church and is not to do double duty. Service is a supplement to generous giving, not a substitute for it. It is as unsatisfactory for one to give service as a substitute for money as to give money as a substitute for service. Besides, whether one's gift is large or small, a full tenth or a portion of it, if it is one's best, no substitute is needed.

5. Is it right to tithe if one cannot pay his bills? One need not wait until he is out of debt before he begins to tithe. Such an approach would be devastating to church budgets! In our generation especially, personal indebtedness is too easy to get into and too hard to get out of. However, God wants no money belonging to someone else, and no check should be written out to the church from funds designated for the light bill. The Christian has an obligation both places, and neither regular church giving nor faithful payments on debts should preclude fulfilling one's duty toward the other.

Such specific questions and answers concerning the practice of tithing may seem to encourage a legalistic approach to churchmanship. I prefer to say that the questions *acknowledge the existence* of such legalistic frames of thought among the laity, while the answers accept people where they are and point them in the directions of broader concepts.

No church has the financial support it requires to do its work well, and the only ultimate solution to the problem is increased giving from the members. However, the tragedy in most situations is not that so few support the church financially but that so many do nothing else. In the preceding chapter we warned of the dangers of too naive an acceptance of the gospel of involvement. Now we must warn that while involvement for its own sake is futile, failure to become involved is fatal. See it in an analogy. Three youths are stranded on an island. They have a limited supply of food and water, but they are within swimming distance of the mainland and home. One dives into the water and frolics aimlessly in it until, weary of his recreation, he climbs back on the island telling the others what fun he had. That is involvement for its own sake. It is pleasant, rejuvenating, and obviously worth while, yet makes no progress toward what should be the main business at hand—crossing the channel that separates him from where he should be living out his life. The second boy dives into the water and heads straight for the mainland, every stroke taking him closer to his destination. It is a long swim and he pulls himself up on the distant shore more weary than rejuvenated, yet filled with the joy of accomplishment and the assurance of reaching home. That is involvement with a purpose. The third youth merely watches the others swim, doing nothing either to reach what must be the final destination of all of them, or to get himself in condition to do so. Completely withdrawing from any involvement, he sets the stage for ultimate starvation if he never leaves the island, or drowning if, with muscles flabby from disuse, he sets out too late to reach the goal. Many laymen take this third stance. They believe in the church and know the importance of doing church work but are reluctant to dive in. Upholding it by their prayers, their presence, and their gifts, they draw the line at contributing any regular or significant service.

The layman's church work in the world, which is his basic service, will be discussed in a later chapter. Here we are thinking of his share of the institutional chores. Normally he will volunteer, or be assigned to tasks for which he has some special skill. However, from time to time he will see the necessity in his house of worship as in the house he occupies with his family, to do jobs simply because they need doing, whether or not he feels any particular competence or interest in them. Small amounts of time devoted to routine or boring chores may add up to a significant service over a period of time. An octogenarian is reported to have spent his eightieth birthday figuring the amount of time he had devoted to various activities in his lifetime and concluded that up to that time he had spent three months scolding children, twice that much time tying neckties, five years waiting for people, and eight full days ordering dogs to stop barking and lie down. I wonder how much time an eighty-year-old churchman with normal concern for the institution with which he has had a life-long relationship might claim to have spent picking up cigarette butts from the front walk or calling people to remind them of meetings. Or, in a somewhat different category, you might find it instructive to figure the probable number of hours that Hazel Benshoff, one of God's living saints, has put into growing flowers, picking them, carting them to the church, and preparing them in breathtakingly beautiful arrangements for the sanctuary where each Sunday they symbolize anew the Resurrection story, and the capacity of all creation to praise God. She has been performing this miracle weekly at The First Methodist Church of Pasadena, California, for over fifty years.

More space than we have would be required if we were to list all of the jobs that need doing in a church. Perhaps it is enough to say that such a list would include everything from dusting pews the custodian missed, or calking leaky windows, to counseling a youth group, or editing the church paper. More church jobs need the thoughtful attention of people who care than most laymen have ever dreamed.

For example, membership on church boards and committees is normally taken too casually. People are assigned to them without being notified of the appointment or after specifically stating that they had little interest or time. Others accept appointment as an honor but exert no effort to learn what the board or committee should do, make no positive contribution to the work being done, and are often missing from key meetings. Still others attend regularly and accept special assignments given to them, but exert no positive leadership. They fail to realize that committee work is a skill to be learned; board membership is an art to be developed. A committee quickly multiplies its effectiveness when the members are given detailed training in what is too often assumed to be inborn knowledge: exactly how a committee—any committee—is supposed to function, how a committee chairman should administer his responsibility, and what individual members can do to make meetings interesting and work productive. A board may be transformed overnight from a series of dull meetings that any alert person who values time will avoid if he can, to an exciting and effective instrument of the church whose meetings wouldn't be missed by anyone wanting to be identified with the most worth-while enterprises. And the miracle is worked by the simple device of requiring every board member to participate in a period of training under skilled leadership in the art of board membership. This should include everything from basic rules of order to methods for steering a bit of legislation through to completion or handling dull or negative personalities. There are some good books on the subject, easily available to laymen who have no opportunity to take a course. These deal with many important things that every board member should know about functions and duties of boards, effective methods of organization, assignment of committees and subcommittees, relationships between officers, staff and members, relationships to other boards and committees and much, much more, including such matters as the political forces that operate within the organization. If more churchmen prepared for their work with care, there would be less need for church administrators to say to them what Paul said to the people in the church in Rome: "I should like to see some results among you, as I have among other Gentiles" (Phillips).

An Englishman visiting in Russia once commented that "Soviet foreign policy is a policy of extreme realism based on total unreality." That's not a bad description of much church organization. The Christian faith is the most realistic thing there is in this age in which propagandists and advertisers have induced so many people to believe a thousand things that aren't so. But how simple-minded and unrealistic we are when we expect to propagate the faith through boards and committees that are ignorant of the basic skills of group dynamics and administrative organization.

After achieving skill in managing the work of the church as an institution, however, the conscientious layman is still troubled with the problem of proportion in the use of his time. One of the most skilled administrators of church boards, committees, and campaigns that I have ever worked with is a man employed with the Rand Corporation, one of the nation's idea organizations, or "think-factories," as they have been dubbed. Involved especially with the military aspects of international relations, his special interest is the relationship of ethics to the use of military power. At the very least, one would have to grant that this is a secular occupation with maximum opportunity for the application of the Christian faith. You can see, therefore, the dilemma faced by this fine churchman. In a letter he wrote to me upon his return from the London Conference on Christian Attitudes Toward Defense and Disarmament, he expressed it this way: "I find that I still have mixed feelings about the administrative side of church work, including such things as campaigns and budgets. Somebody has to do it, and I want to do my share. But our discussions at camp last summer about 'God's Colony in Man's World' left me with the feeling that the most significant work is 'out there' outside of the colony. And to go 'out there' in the area that I feel called to try to penetrate if I can (ethics and military power), I must first qualify myself. This takes time and more time. All the while, back in the 'colony,' there is work to be done, and this is where the dilemma arises: How much time and energy should go to maintaining the colony and how much to getting ready to go out into the world? If you ever find a nice clean-cut answer to that one, let me know."

I have no clean-cut answer to it. All I know for sure is that both jobs must be done, and for the sake of his own soul, if nothing else, every layman should have a part in both enterprises. Proportions will have to be left up to the individual. However excited he may be about the challenge "out there," he must not forget the demands of the daily chores at home or the importance of knowing his own assignment and fulfilling it faithfully.

To do this, he should know the rules and obey them in spirit.

Few things foul up the institutional machinery—which, as we have noted, is not the evil thing it is often assumed to be—more quickly than ignorance of its construction and intended operation. No mechanic should be asked to use a complicated machine, take advantage of its virtues, and keep it in working order unless he is familiar with its parts and their relationships, its weaknesses, idiosyncrasies, and areas most likely to give trouble. He should be shown how to operate the machine so as to get maximum results with the least wear or risk of accident and should be warned of its limitations so that he will not be disappointed in its failure to do what it was never intended to accomplish.

If in the last two sentences of the preceding paragraph, beginning with the words, "No mechanic," the word "layman" is substituted for "mechanic" and "church organization" for "machine," you will have sound counsel for the churchman. He must know the rules by which his church is governed if he is to find satisfaction in its work. Most denominations have a rule book of some kind, but the average layman has never seen it. Many local churches have a set of by-laws defining the straight and narrow path to which they are committed, but few indeed are they who find it. If they do get possession of such a document, the chances are good that it is out of date and what rules they learn from it are the wrong ones. Local Methodist churches do not customarily have a set of by-laws in addition to the Methodist Discipline, which applies equally to all local churches in the Methodist denomination. However, about six months after becoming minister of one church I discovered the existence of such a set of regulations one day at a meeting of the board of trustees, when a fine attorney who believed in strict adherence to the rules governing any organization with which he was connected, quoted from it. A few questions on my part revealed the fact that this was the document to which members of the board were accustomed to turn for guidance. I managed to locate a copy in the office files and discovered that it had been prepared twenty-five years earlier, based on the rules of the denomination as enunciated in the Methodist Discipline of that year. Although the Discipline had been revised, in some instances drastically, six different times during that period, the local by-laws never had. Not only at the time they join the church, but repeatedly thereafter, laymen should be given the opportunity to learn the rules so that they will be in a position to use them as they were intended to be used, to do Christ's work on earth.

Such use involves wise interpretation of the rules. That is why I have suggested not only that laymen should know the rules governing their church but that they should obey them in spirit. Rigid enslavement to the machine makes one indistinguishable from it and as mechanical as the machine itself. This is true whether one is referring to machinery of whirling wheels and outstretched conveyor belts or the machinery of church organization. That is why obedience to the rules must not be unconditional. It must be obedience "in spirit."

This may appear to give members a dangerous degree of latitude. Is it not true that persons granted considerable freedom in interpreting rules will eventually disregard them and lose all sense of their authority? If you don't follow "the book" absolutely, why follow it at all? These are good questions, and there are some good answers.

For one thing, law itself is not as rigid as some people suppose. Laws are not absolute. That is why courts spend so much time interpreting them. Law is an emergent thing, constantly in process of growth. This applies to church law as readily as to civil law.

The church is not a rigid organization. It is flexible and in process of development. Accordingly, a rule which was both important and helpful last year may be quite harmful if strictly applied to the changed organization as it exists today. I remember reading that Methodist Bishop Gerald Ensley wrote a reference to the fact that the church is more like a plant than a building and that working with it requires more of the skills appropriate to agriculture than to architecture. Thus the rules must be interpreted in a manner which allows for and encourages growth.

It is much easier to be rigid than to be flexible in these matters. Absolutism leaves little room for debate. Discussion becomes unnecessary since the rule book saves the members of the organization from the pain of decision making. Besides, you have to trust people if you are granting them the privilege of interpreting the spirit as opposed to the letter of the law. It is better that way. A few will take advantage of the latitude to do what they should not be doing and what the law of the church, if strictly interpreted, would have prevented, but little is lost. These are the same ones who, if confined to the letter of the law, would take advantage of a technicality, however unreasonable it might appear to those accustomed to applying common sense.

Fortunately, the letter and the spirit of church law are seldom in conflict, so the problem has to do with exceptional cases only. It is a good policy to follow the rules with reasonable exactness when there is no important reason for doing otherwise. Whenever legal transactions are involved, the law of the church should be followed in meticulous detail. This is not only the right thing for law-abiding citizens to do, but it is good insurance against future difficulty at the hands of some die-hard who doesn't like the action taken and has no scruples against raising a fuss. In legal matters there is very little room for choosing the spirit as opposed to the letter of the law unless clearance to do so has been given by an authorized denominational official or a decision of the court. Written documents attesting thereto should be safely preserved.

There remain a number of instances where cooperation with the law's intent is a better attitude of approach than strict adherence to the law's demand. A few examples: If the church law requires an offering for student work on a given Sunday of the year, the local church should assume the freedom to write an appropriate amount into the annual budget or receive the offering on a different date, if student work will be better served by such a shift. If church law limits the education committee of the church to fifteen members, but there are very good local reasons why there should be seventeen people named, then seventeen there should be. It's a matter of developing a feeling for the thing. Good laymen know the rules of their church and obey them in spirit.

A mature layman will also learn to know the context in which his church stands and he will seek to keep the relationships strong.

Denominational loyalties are not as firm as they once were, and there is a tendency for Protestants to jump denominational fences with neither injury nor exertion. They just ask for a transfer and the gate opens. Most people are more loyal to their political party than to their denomination.

These weakening denominational loyalties are generally considered to be a sign of growth, indicating broad-mindedness and a tendency for the churches to be less sectarian. Whatever the gains, there are also some losses, not the least of which is ignorance of the history, polity, and theological posture of the denomination of which one's local church is a part. Or, if not ignorance of these things, at least the absence of any sense of belonging to a particular stream of history or speaking from a definite theological tradition. It is as though the denominations, like broken strings of beads, had been thrown into one bag and shaken until the beads have fallen from the strings. The separate beads may still be identifiable as having come from a certain string, but the relationship no longer binds them. Indeed, they may fit well with other beads from other strings. Denominational intermarriage has been going on so long that, religiously speaking, hardly anyone can claim ecclesiastical purity anymore. On the ecumenical scene, mixed parentage has practically become a prestige symbol while denominational purists nurse inferiority complexes.

Clearly, denominational loyalties are not as strong as they once were. As a result, individual church members have a declining awareness of being a part of or loyal to anything bigger than their local church. Ecumenicity started out to give the individual member of the local church a sense of being a part of something bigger than his denomination: Christendom in toto. Results to date appear to have stimulated the reverse process. Instead of expanding beyond his denomination, he has retreated from it. With loyalty largely confined to whatever local church claims his current affiliation, he pays little attention to the denomination as a whole unless it embarrasses him by making the news with a social stand in opposition to his own. As for any pride in being a part of the Council of Churches, local, national or world, he is quick to say that it does not represent him; it misrepresents him.

For a long while now, denominational and interdenominational leaders have been widening the gap between themselves and John Q. Churchman. They do more talking about grass-roots movements than do those who *are* the grass-roots. This may be an expression of nostalgia, fear, or guilt. But if they ever dig into the earth themselves it is only to sample the soil. They do not grow there, and they do not know the sharp-edged feel of the other blades of grass that cut across them when the strong winds blow, or what it is to wilt when weeds take root nearby. Their interest in the local scene is no doubt genuine, but their understanding of it is up for question. Pursuing what Samuel H. Miller calls "the false infinite of a superficial collectivity," they forget that "truth is no truer in the aggregate of humanity than it is in the heart of one person. The eternal is not created or achieved by universal agreement."

I am an organizational man myself, if you will grant a thoroughly constructive meaning in the term. I love my denomination, I believe in it, and give my cooperation to it. Most of its official stands on public issues have my enthusiastic support and those that don't, I understand. And I'm a Council of Churches man besides, believing in it at all its levels. If the Council wants someone to speak in their behalf, then I'm their boy. Which is precisely the reason I'm heated up about this thing. I want those competent, far-sighted, Christian scholars and statesmen who operate at the highest levels of denominational and interdenominational life to know that they are not communicating. The message isn't getting through. God knows the gap is great enough between the minister (with his theological education, idealistic ideas on social issues, and his blundering in practical matters of church business) and the rank and file of his membership. But this is nothing to compare with the chasm to be crossed before the average layman sees the National Council of Churches as essential to his religious life. Not many laymen are really excited about their denomination. They accept it because it is tied in some mysterious way to their local church, a comprehensible organizational unit for which they do have a measure of affection. If it is not ignored, it is as apt to be seen as an enemy as it is a friend. Big, impersonal, authoritarian, it has a reputation for sucking the blood out of local churches, stealing their minister just when they are getting to know him, and speaking for them in the press when they would much rather speak for themselves. As for the Council of Churches, it tends to be either hated or ignored. Even its professed friends have scant time to give to it. The others feign a spirit of support because cooperation is supposed to be proper, pretend or forget that it exists except for those irritating moments when it asks for money or makes one of those radical pronouncements it is famous for, or fume in anger over its audacity in claiming a relationship with all the major denominations and their constituent churches and members who would much prefer a less friendly association.

Here is a real job for the conscientious layman. Let him learn the exciting history of his denomination, understand its unique contribution to Christian life and thought, get acquainted with its heroes past and present until he identifies with all of them and feels himself a part, beyond all chance of any separation, of the noble things his church has come to mean. Let him learn about the Council, how it came to be, and whom it represents and what it plans to do. Let him stay with this, until he sees himself as part of this mosaic whose awesome beauty he will no more deny. Let him trace the streams of theological thought from where they start to their converging place and far beyond, and let him submerge himself in them until he too is caught by the irresistible pull of the sea and knows that he is a part of something big and moving and fresh and powerful, from which he could never separate himself nor want to. Let him find out who he is as he relates to all that he's a part of. Churchmanship requires a man to know the context in which his church is set and to keep the relationships strong. This will take some sacrifice. It will mean more than study only. It will involve attendance at conferences, participation in interfaith "dialogue" (there's that word again) and planned efforts to get the strongest members of one's local church participating too. It means more time, more money, more effort, more meetings. But it's worth it all, and it's the only way.

X

The Layman and His Minister

Organizations must have leaders. The church has many of them. Chief among them in the local church is the minister or, in the case of a multiple staff, the senior minister.

Ernest Fremont Tittle was the senior minister of The First Methodist Church, Evanston, Illinois, throughout the years of World War II. Known as a social prophet, his accent was on world peace, and while the country was at war, he continued to remind his Evanston congregation that armed conflict was not God's way of handling human differences. His sermons drew fire, and efforts were made to silence him. One man, determined to get the famous preacher out of Evanston, sought the support of one of the church's laymen. But the churchman declined, saying, "Years ago when my wife died and my world fell to pieces and I walked all night along the lake shore, my minister, without my ever asking him, walked all night beside me. He can say whatever he believes and I will listen."

That simple incident forms the portrait of a great preacher and a great layman. It shows a preacher who combines the tender heart of a shepherd with the daring tongue of a prophet and a layman who honors his minister and defends his church. It takes courage for a preacher to speak out in the face of opposition, and it takes courage for a layman to stand by his preacher when the tides are running against him. Such tenderness, daring, honor, and courage are the building blocks for the strong relationships that so often exist between laymen and their minister.

Ministers and laymen can become the best of personal friends. I can testify to that. It is hopeless for me to try to call the roll of the men and women in the churches I have served whose lives have touched my own in a meaningful way and whom I shall always think of not as "laymen" or members of such and such a church, but as my friends. These good people are scattered over this world and into the next. They are of different races, ages, occupations, and strata of society. Some I see frequently. Some I have not seen for years. It does not matter. Speaking the same language, seeking the same goals, and following the same Master, we have too much in common ever to be severed in spirit.

Each of these friendships has a different history. Some were naturals from the start, as like-minded people quickly discover and understand one another. Some can be traced to a tragic or other deeply meaningful experience that was shared. Others blossomed slowly through a succession of everyday experiences. After years of planning programs together, raising budgets together, commenting on political developments, inquiring about the family, checking on proposed plans, and hammering out those details that are the inconspicuous stepping stones of progress, a consciousness of valued friendships emerged. This, incidentally, is one of the rewards of a long pastorate. It is a pity that so many ministers never stay long enough in one place to come to know any of the laymen really well.

However, even in long pastorates, a minister will not build close relationships with all of his laymen. This is partly due to temperamental differences, but it is also a simple matter of mathematics. In a church of four thousand members, for example, the minister won't even recognize a large percentage of his people if he meets them on the street, and many of them will fail to take the initiative to get acquainted with him. There is a report of one minister who, traveling by plane, was drawn into conversation with the hostess. Noting the designation of "Reverend" on his ticket, she was pleased to learn that he was of the same denomination as she. You can imagine the consternation of both of them, however, when he mentioned the name of the large city church of which he was the senior minister and she exclaimed, "Oh, my gracious! You're my pastor!"

It often happens, as in this case, that a minister knows so little about some members of his church that he wouldn't recognize them if he met them in the air. Yet, they feel quite close to him, speak of him often, and think of him as a personal friend. There is a reason for this. Every week the laymen see their minister and hear him speak. They come to know his personality, to understand his thoughts, and to share his convictions. They read his column in the church paper, and spot news of him in the secular press as quickly and with as much sense of personal involvement as news items about members of their own family.

Meanwhile he has had a chance to establish such personal identification with very few of his laymen. This puts him at a disadvantage, and he is sometimes caught by surprise when they express a strong feeling of affection or censure (as one does toward those he knows best) when he doesn't even know who they are. Ministers of large churches are especially familiar with this problem as it relates to the elderly women who are found in such abundance in their congregations, and who look so distressingly alike. Coming as I do from the city that inspired the phrase, "The little old lady from Pasadena," I can speak with some authority about this. I can also testify to the fact that once the "little old ladies" are sorted out, they are likely to surprise one with their charm and wit. The sensitive minister is quick to recognize that long before he has individualized these people, they have him identified, classified, and pigeonholed. He should therefore be prepared for them to react to him in a very definite manner, and he should appreciate the close personal feelings that these reactions reflect, even if he is in no position to return them.

In time the feelings will be shared and close human bonds will be felt both ways. Rich friendships will develop. This is as it should be, although there are those who object to such close ties between the ordained and the unordained. Ministers are often advised to develop their personal friendships outside the local church, preferably with other clergymen. It is supposed that a friendship with one layman will stimulate jealousy in another, or that laymen coming to know their minister well will lose respect for him. It is also suggested that laymen who develop a close personal friendship with a minister are likely to wield more than their share of influence over him or that they will find it hard to be loyal to his successor.

There is some truth in all this, but the approach is too negative. Laymen are not a minister's "clients" or "customers" or "patients," with whom he must maintain a strict professional relationship. They are his friends. They are his brothers and sisters in Christ. An intelligent minister should be able to get close to his laymen without allowing himself and his conscience to be owned by them. He should develop deep relationships without building exclusive ones. There is something inhuman about a minister who can share others' sorrows, aspirations, disappointments, doubts, fears, hopes, and religious faith without coming to love them as members of his family.

Sentimentalism should be avoided, of course, for while sentiment is strong with intelligent feeling, sentimentalism gets sloppy. G. K. Chesterton defined the difference in a way we can understand when he said that while "sentiment is jam on your bread, sentimentalism is jam on your face."

Sentimentally based relationships are candy bridges, sweet but incapable of supporting the traffic. Relationships based on honest sentiment are steel-strong. They can carry a heavy load of the important ideas and emotions that properly pass between human beings. Such bridges should be built between laymen and ministers because each is vital to the other, each needs the other for his own fulfillment.

The importance of the minister to the layman is apparent in the fact that the minister is the official representative of the layman's religion. His hand rests on the layman's head in baptism and passes him the elements in the Sacrament of the Lord's Supper. His voice intones the layman's wedding vows, reads "the word of God" to him each Sunday, and preaches the gospel he knows to be the bread of life. His presence with the layman's family at the time of sorrow suggests the presence of Christ; his counsel in the hour of trouble gives confidence in the leading of a divine power. Associated with the most vital experiences of his life, the minister is clearly of major importance to the layman.

And laymen are important to the minister. His entire career rests in their hands. They name his salary, furnish his residence, and sometimes discipline his children. Their generosity determines the statistical record with which he closes his church year. Their reaction to his wife affects his domestic happiness, and their response to his sermons does much to determine his professional success or failure. If the minister is an authority figure to the laymen in terms of eternal things, the laymen are authority figures to the minister in terms of worldly things.

The fact that ministers and laymen are important to each other may seem obvious, but it is a truth to be underlined because people who are important to each other powerfully affect one another. Each becomes for the other the focus of attention, the subject of conversation, the source of satisfaction, or the symbol of disappointment. Each is capable of arousing intense feeling in the other. That is why a discussion of lay-ministerial relationships is necessary.

Some people say that these relationships are no different from any other form of human association. These are the compulsive debunkers whose greatest delight is in proving that all men are of one flesh and equally subject to it. They are the first to call the minister by his first name, put him in a bathing suit, or make him the clown at the church carnival. That is quite all right if he wishes to cooperate. If he is capable and self-confident, he is not dependent upon special titles and he does not worry about losing caste by exposing his bunions or appearing as a clown. Yet there is a problem here. The problem is with the layman who feels inferior until he has peeled the dignity from his preacher, who wants the minister to be no different from himself.

But there are differences. However much they hold in common, ministers are not laymen and laymen are not ministers. Consequently, laymen relate to ministers differently from the way they relate to one another. There is nothing wrong with this. A man's relationship to his wife is different from his relationship to his children, and his approach to his boss differs from his approach to his employees. This does not mean he is a hypocrite. It indicates only that he is adaptable, and understands that what is appropriate in one relationship may be very inappropriate in another.

It is not enough, however, for the layman's relationship to his minister to be unique. It must be unique in the right way. It must be natural. Unfortunately, many laymen relate unnaturally to their minister. Holding some stereotype idea of what he should be like, they relate to him as though he personified the stereotype. He doesn't, he can't, and he shouldn't. Until realism replaces fantasy in their thinking, laymen will have strained relationships with their minister.

To see the problem clearly, let's examine some of the most common poses laymen assume in relation to the clergy. First, there are the *idolaters*. Some people—more women than men—tend to worship their preacher. Their attitude toward him corresponds with their attitude toward God. It takes the form of adoration. With some it is a physical attraction and comes in the category of a "crush." With others it is the result of lifelong training that ministers are something special or the irrational conclusion that the minister is the embodiment of the ideals he preaches. But whatever its source, it goes beyond the limits of "due respect" to become a fawning adulation that makes normal human relationships impossible. It is unhealthy both for the layman and for the minister.

It encourages laymen to become dependent, to ask their minister to make decisions for them which they should be making for themselves, to accept his beliefs without examining them, and his attitudes without submitting them to appropriate evaluation. It sets the stage for disillusionment. The laymen who thinks that his minister, though somewhat less than divine, is somewhat more than human, is in for a jolt. Idols crumble.

Unfortunately, some ministers encourage adulation. They like having worshipers. To be accepted as an authority feeds their ego, and to be cast in a father role, often by people twice their own age, develops their taste for power. It spawns an ugly disrespect for the adulthood of others and a tendency to encourage their immaturities.

It also nourishes the immaturities of the minister himself. If he becomes addicted to being adored, his actions will be calculated to secure the desired reaction. He will make fewer bold administrative decisions because he doesn't want to run the risk of tarnishing the image. Selling his soul for a spurious security, he will submit to the wishes of whatever laymen fill the leadership vacuum he has created, and his sermons, progressively shorn of anything which might upset some worshiper, will be reduced to sweet homilies on kindness. Thus the wheel of fate will turn, and the man on whom the laymen leaned will be leaning on the laymen. It is unhealthy for both ministers and laymen to become neurotically dependent upon one another.

By contrast, a wholesome relationship is one in which each helps the other to stand on his own feet. In such a relationship the minister encourages the layman to think for himself and to build a faith that is not dependent upon a priestly figure nearby to hold it together. And the layman encourages the minister to speak the truth as he sees it without fear of being rejected tomorrow by the laymen who praised him yesterday. When laymen see that they can honestly evaluate their minister as a person without losing their respect for his high office as a clergyman, they are setting the stage for minister-layman relationships that are vibrant with interacting ideas and productive endeavor.

A good time for this realistic approach to begin is with the arrival of each new minister. Either the minister or the laymen can take the initiative. One of the first things I did in one church to which I was appointed was to invite a group of about twenty leading laymen to my home for an evening's discussion. I explained that I had a clear-cut idea of my function as the senior minister of their church but that it was important to know whether my understanding of this corresponded with theirs. So I asked one question: "What do you understand my job to be?" They talked freely and expressed definite concepts which one member of the group wrote down. When they had finished, I expressed my convictions on the matter which, to the delight of all of us, corresponded almost exactly with theirs. That got us off to a good start. Whether I lived up to what they expected of me and what I expected of myself is an open question. But we were agreed upon our goal. That gave us common ground to stand on and saved us from many possible misunderstandings.

As laymen come to understand the work of the minister, realism replaces fantasy and adoration becomes unnecessary.

Even more important, however, is for the laymen to understand their own calling. I sometimes think that lay adoration of the clergy is nothing but frustrated creativity. Religious people want to be involved in a noble venture, and if they don't know what else to do, they turn their loving attention on the man whose office symbolizes the good qualities they would like to have and the good things they would like to do. The current emphasis on the ministry of the laity should do much to correct the tendency of some laymen to focus their attention too exclusively and adoringly on the minister.

A second type of laymen to be found in our churches are the *patrons*. The patronizing attitude is most likely to be assumed by persons of wealth or influence. They like to "sponsor" their preacher and take pride in thinking of him as their boy. He becomes their protégé. Ministers often warm up to this kind of relationship, just as they warm up to those who adore them. People with a patronizing attitude can finance some of the minister's pet projects, send him on a tour of the Holy Land, and introduce him to opportunities that might not otherwise be open to him. If the lay "patron" is a genuinely mature person who recognizes unusual quality in his minister, and who is fortunate enough to have the means to help him develop his potentiality to the fullest extent, but who has no desire to control the preacher, this kind of relationship can be solid and positive. Many ministers have been made great because of the wise guidance and generous gifts of individual laymen. But if the patron has more wealth than stability, and is using his generosity as a means of buying friendship or exercising power, the relationship is unwholesome and should be broken before it demoralizes both of them.

Frequently, patronizing is humiliating to the supposed beneficiary. One minister found it to be so and asked, "Am I the shepherd of my flock or its pet lamb?"

Generosity is appreciated, of course, but it should always be extended in such a way as to enhance, not to destroy the beneficiary's self-respect. For example, if a physician offers his services without charge because the church is not paying the minister enough to live on, this is humiliating. If he does the same thing as a professional courtesy such as he extends to his fellow physicians, this adds to the minister's stature. There is no reason why church members, either individually or collectively, may not give their minister a Christmas gift, buy him a new car, or send him on a trip around the world. But let them do these things as expressions of their high regard for him, or as a way of making his ministry more effective. Let them never extend these kindnesses in a patronizing way.

There is more involved here than the feelings of individual clergymen. To be patronizing in one's attitude toward a particular minister is to belittle the ministry. For the Christian, the church is the greatest of all institutions and deserves the highest quality of leadership that can be found. Consequently, any layman who treats his minister as his pet charity reveals a hidden disdain for the church. He may be regular in his attendance and generous in his giving, but these virtues are no substitute for respect. If he is condescending in his attitude toward ministers, the integrity of his own dedication to the church should be examined.

This may be tested by his attitude toward the possibility of his own son entering the ministry. Not everyone's children should be ministers or missionaries, but laymen who support other people's sons and daughters in such lives of Christian dedication while looking for something "better" for their own are revealing a patronizing attitude toward the church and all its leadership. This is demoralizing. In the Christian church none can afford the luxury of being sponsors of others. We are co-workers in God's vineyard.

This is not to say that ministers could not use considerable special help from laymen who see the need and wish to be helpful. The best thing they can do, however, is to create in the church the kind of climate of opinion and management of organization that enables each minister to grow to his full stature. The layman who wants to be helpful to his minister can help him most by making it possible for him to succeed at the job that is uniquely his. The chance to succeed in one's chosen vocation is a greater gift than paternalistically extended favors designed to make vocational failure palatable.

A third attitude which a layman may take toward his minister is that of the *critic*. Whether this is rooted in a friendly or an unfriendly relationship, it expresses a feeling of superiority. It carries the assumption that the layman is an adequate judge of what a preacher should be, and that the preacher will benefit from the layman's wise counsel. For such a layman, the preacher is not a man of God whose words are to be heeded, but an employee of the congregation whose work is to be perfected. At its worst, the ensuing criticism is vicious and designed to destroy. At its best, it is thoughtful, and genuinely helpful. Most of it, falling between these two extremes, is little more than the expression of some minor personal bias.

Ministers, being public figures and representatives of institutionalized religion, are natural targets for human hostilities. Paranoid personalities and others of a suspicious nature are bound to attack them. They attract criticism by the nature of their vocation. Most of this criticism is of the crackpot variety. In language betraying the most intense feeling, the minister may be denounced for his "grinning photograph" in the parish paper, a misinterpretation of the most innocuous thing he said in his last sermon, or his failure to call on someone who isn't in his church and who he didn't know was sick. Any comment he makes on a social issue is likely to draw fire. One Monday morning I received two letters in response to the previous day's radio broadcast. One took me to task for being too liberal, the other for being too conservative. Both letters were reactions to the same sermon. Both quoted the same illustration in the sermon as proof of their points. Neither one understood what I was trying to say. This may be nothing more than evidence of my inability to make things clear. Or it may be an illustration of the fact that many people are looking for someone to criticize and the minister is a convenient target.

A minister in the Midwest told me that one of his laymen had called him a Communist. He couldn't see what had provoked such an accusation, so he asked one of his leading members why this fellow would have said such a thing. The man answered, "What he really wanted to say was that you were a Democrat, but he didn't want to go that far." There is no question but that ministers are subjected to a good deal of crackpot criticism.

They are also criticized by some sociologists, theologians, educators, and other learned men and women. These people tell them they are irrelevant to what is going on in the world and that no one listens to what they have to say. This is usually intelligent criticism and should be carefully examined. However, since nobody whips a dead horse, the vigor of these attacks belies the point they try to make. If the ministry is as irrelevant as some of them say, why does it arouse such intense feelings in them? It appears to loom so large in their lives that, like youth seeking psychological independence from their parents, they continue their barrage of accusation. This troubles the ministers who, like parents under attack from their offspring, are keenly aware of their own shortcomings.

The minister is further criticized by the rank and file membership of his church. Some of this comes from top leaders who are expressing their need for more ministerial assistance. Some comes from the uninformed who are expressing their ignorance. Some comes from the overworked who are expressing their weariness. And some comes from honest seekers-after-truth and spiritual soundness who are not receiving as much help from their minister as they have been led to believe they have a right to expect. Most of these criticisms are more or less minor in themselves, but piled up they constitute a considerable weight on a minister's shoulders.

This is a fact of life which every minister needs to accept. Like a politician, he must learn to live with criticism or crack up. Any attempt to answer every critic—to say nothing of efforts to adjust his life and ministry to meet each critic's demands—would consume his time, make his nerves jumpy, and his character hollow. Consequently, it is a great day in the life of a minister when he learns that he can't please everybody, and in the life of the laymen when they learn it isn't his business to try. Any preacher who is unwilling to risk opposition for the sake of the gospel has no business in a Christian pulpit. Any layman who deserts his minister when he is under fire adds little dignity to the pew.

In relating to their minister, laymen should remember that most people do not need someone to tell them what to do and how to do it as much as they need someone to believe in them. We all know that nagging is a thoroughly destructive form of human behavior, yet we cling to the fiction that there is something called "constructive criticism" that is the source of good. The truth is, however, that even so-called "helpful criticism" is generally more critical than helpful. Candor in human relations is to be encouraged. Ministers and laymen should be able to communicate with one another in honesty. But this is to be distinguished from that sometimes psychologically endorsed form of cruelty that is too graciously called "frankness," and that is supposed to drain off feelings of hostility and open the gates of loving communication. It does nothing of the sort. I have seen it tried many times, usually under the banner of "honesty," and I am ready to testify that it generates more hostility than it evaporates. Turning the other cheek, returning good for evil, and praying for those who hate or despise us have always been better therapy than unlocking the urge to be primitive. It will ever be so.

In church as elsewhere, criticism is a confession of the inadequacy and insecurity of the critic more than a description of the shortcomings of the criticized. It is never an expression of our love for one another. It may express fear or anger or hatred or disgust or frustration or envy or impatience, but not love. Love accepts the beloved as he now is, not as he might be if he took our advice. Indeed, if I can have the love of my children or my congregation only as I deserve it, then I shall never have it. Their love is much too precious a thing for me ever to be worthy of it. My only hope is that they may love me as I am, while yet a sinner. That's the way I should love them: with praise, not criticism. I must support them on their weak side and praise them wherein they are strong. All of us, ministers and laymen alike, should acknowledge our imperfections and go on from there.

It is said that a group of Oxford dons once wrote a letter to Queen Victoria, inviting her to visit Oxford. They began their letter, "Conscious as we are of our shortcomings . . ." One of the men wasn't sure of the accuracy of this statement, however, and suggested it ought to read, "Conscious as we are of one another's shortcomings. . . ." Both ministers and laymen should try to be more conscious of their own shortcomings, and less conscious of the other fellow's. They should develop the spirit of the elderly clergyman who, the morning after his first sermon in a new parish, was greeted by one of the women of the church who declared, "I think you are an old fool." This didn't upset him. He merely answered, "There's no doubt about it. I've known it for years. What's your evidence?" That disarmed her and she became manageable. And as Robert Rodenmayer, who tells the story, comments: "The point of the story is, of course, that the man was speaking the precise truth. He *was* an old fool. God uses fools to get his work done; He doesn't have anybody else. A Christian is a redeemed fool."

In Gregory Wilson's *The Stained Glass Jungle,* one minister, concluding that he was not good enough to be preaching the gospel, confessed his sins to a brother minister who pointed out that there is a mixture of good and evil in all of us and asked, "Who's gonna be left to proclaim truth and right in this world, if not some imperfect human like you or me?" And then he added, "Maybe God has to pick up a crooked stick to strike with now and then, if all the nice clean shiny straight ones are too flimsy for the job." He has a good point. Certainly every minister should seek to personify the Christian life he preaches. But even when he has done his best to achieve perfection, there remain flaws in his character which anyone attracted to that sort of endeavor can probably discover and magnify for all to see. But this is a questionable way for a layman to spend his time. He is called to something nobler than to be the preacher's critic.

That brings us to a fourth attitude which some laymen hold toward their minister. It is the attitude of an *enemy*. Occasionally a layman sets himself in solid opposition to his preacher. For any one of a number of reasons—a personality clash, a misunderstanding, a theological difference—the layman seeks to discredit his minister and, if possible, have him moved to another parish.

I have known laymen whose chief delight was harpooning preachers. They felt their calling was to defend the church against any leader who promised progress. If their minister arose in a board meeting to propose a forward move, they could be depended upon to take the opposite stand, and if the church seemed to be inclined to move in the direction indicated by the minister, they organized for battle, called their reserves into action, and packed the next meeting with their recruits, many of whom were so raw they didn't know what the battle was about. But they loved a good fight. Sometimes ministers deserve to be opposed, and the most thoughtful laymen may determine that a change in ministerial leadership would be to the benefit of all involved. Even then the situation should be handled with loving concern for the minister as a person. No layman is required to destroy a minister's self-confidence or reputation in order to get him moved.

Nor should ministers feel unnecessary enmity toward laymen. Unfortunately, some ministers see their laymen as antagonists with whom they expect to do battle, just as some laymen wait for their minister to propose a forward move so that they can oppose it. I once knew a minister whose greatest sense of accomplishment was in fighting his laymen. He never felt he was doing anything unless he had stimulated some group in the church to go after his hide.

A lay-ministerial relationship that is based on antagonism is intolerable. There is too much important work to be done for co-workers to waste their energies in conflict with one another. Perhaps there was a time when the church could afford the luxury of internal dissension, but we cannot afford it now. "How do you like the new minister?" is no longer the pertinent question for laymen to ask, and ministers have more important work to do than to seek to secure their popularity by coddling temperamental laymen, who, if not appeased, will be active enemies.

This is not to overlook the fact that creative tension is the condition of growth and that if church people don't cross one another now and then church life becomes sterile. Conflicts intelligently and lovingly resolved give more evidence of abundant life than the kind of agreement that comes because no one proposes anything worth fighting about, or because one party always buckles under.

In a pointed article entitled, "Why the Sniping at Our Preachers?" Milburn P. Akers, editor of the *Chicago Sun-Times*, writes:

> I am not one who believes clergymen should be immune from criticism . . .
>
> I am, however, one who has wearied of the frequently uninformed, many times baseless, sometimes downright vituperative attacks on clergymen and churches—especially when such attacks result from pastors and

church groups speaking out on the social ills of our time. I am convinced that such attacks can only harm Protestantism by undermining the faith and confidence of churchmen in their chosen spokesmen and institutions.

No segment of American society—not even the church—should expect its activities in controversial areas to go unchallenged. But neither our churches nor our nation can afford strife of the kind which breeds mutual mistrust.

. . . I do not say, nor do I intend to imply, that opinions and activities of all Protestant clergymen deserve universal approval. I doubt there is a minister in the country whose judgment I could support 100 percent of the time.

. . . I am something of a pragmatist, myself. Occasionally, I agree with the liberals; sometimes I agree with the conservatives; much of the time I agree only with myself. But I have lived long enough to discover that I am sometimes wrong, that those with whom I occasionally disagree are sometimes right. The clash of ideas is essential in a free society. If divergent ideas—even unpopular ideas—cannot be expressed, the society is no longer free. The clash of ideas is jeopardized when sincere, informed persons, whether of liberal or conservative persuasion, lay or clergy, are vilified because they hold dissenting or unpopular views.

. . . In his role of prophet for his church and community, the clergyman has a duty to speak out for what he feels are needed reforms of the national and community life.

I am not suggesting that clergymen should espouse a particular point of view. I am merely stating that a clergyman . . . has at least as much right, and probably

> more obligation, to express opinions on the moral and social problems of the day as any other individual, association, or organization.
>
> . . . The Protestant clergy, individually and collectively, are a well-educated, dedicated, spiritually motivated lot, who, thank God, seek to activate America's social conscience. What they need from laymen is not heckling but support based on understanding.[1]

This layman has said it better than I can. Laymen who snipe at their preacher as at an enemy are themselves enemies of the common good.

A fifth attitude a layman may take toward his minister is that of a *competitor*. The minister is automatically in a place of leadership, and as such he is a threat to any layman who plays, or hopes to play, a dominant role in the church's life. A layman may compete with the minister for popularity as a speaker, or even as the darling of the congregation. He is more likely to compete for dominance in decision-making. Some laymen are quite willing to let the minister be the church's "voice" if they can function as its "brain."

Others compete as the "voice." Some musicians, for example. When they challenge the order of service, which is as clearly the minister's responsibility as anything in the life of the church, they are usually exerting influence beyond their area of competence. Few of them recognize good liturgical practice when they see it, make their judgments largely from the standpoint of musical performance, which is a different matter. This sometimes becomes evident when they are asked to sing while the offering is being received. Those who do not understand the liturgical reasons for this or who do not have the "feel" for the totality of the worship service are likely to respond by asking the minister how he would like to preach a sermon while ushers are

[1] *In Together,* March 1962, pp. 14 ff.

receiving the offering. This reveals two errors in thinking. The first is that sermons and anthems (or solos) serve the same purpose in an order of service as sermons and should be handled in an identical manner; and two, that vocal numbers in a church service are basically concert performances and should be treated as such.

This is not true. When church music can maintain the standards of the best secular concert music one may be grateful, but it is imperative that church musicians fully understand that an anthem, for example, is not to be thought of as a concert number. It is an offering to God, appropriately sung while the offering plates are being passed. This is important in the total experience of worship. The alternative is an organ "offertory" which seldom serves any function but to mark time until the chord is struck for the Doxology. It is almost always a time when worshipers' minds wander and their eyes dully follow the irregular progress of the offering plate or delineate the curious outline of some design in a stained glass window. It is lost time. But in churches in which musicians are more concerned with the movement and effectiveness of the total service of worship than the concert-effectiveness of each musical number, this dull period is magnificently redeemed with great music.

Teachers of adult Sunday-school classes and counselors of youth groups also sometimes compete with the minister. This is evident among the former when they use their classroom as a pulpit for propounding doctrines contrary to those preached by the minister, and among the latter if they show signs of jealousy when the youth turn to the minister with their confidences instead of to them. Similar competition often shows up among church treasurers and others dealing with financial matters if the minister's counsel on fiscal affairs carries more weight with the board members than theirs. Many such persons become rigid in their demands and sound the alarm of pending financial ruin, not because the church is in any such danger, but because they are losing control of church financial policy. They are competing with the minister for power, and losing.

Part of the problem here is the absence of well-established and thoroughly understood rules of procedure such as exist to an extreme degree in the military and more moderately in business and industry. In these instances, lines of authority are clearly drawn, priorities specifically established, and job descriptions made perfectly plain. Every effort is made to pinpoint responsibility and to grant authority commensurate with it. All this is done imperfectly, of course, but in the army, no private, like a choir member in church, seeks to tell the General when he will or when he won't perform his assigned duty. And in industry, no bookkeeper who values his job, will, like some church treasurers in relation to the minister, seek to tell top management what their policies are to be.

The church, of course, is different from industry and the army, and while it may need to be more like them in some matters involving efficiency, in other ways it will never be like them. This is not a handicap but an opportunity. The church is a brotherhood. It places a high value on all persons, whatever their positions. It grants the right of the newest, humblest member to speak about top administration or anything else. Such a wide-open system can lead to the kinds of inappropriate actions already described, or it can lead to a warm human fellowship that loses nothing in efficiency because of its willingness to listen to everybody. Properly functioning, it is a society of people who never compete with one another because they are never threatened by one another. Choir members feel free to ask questions about the order of service because they are eager to learn, but they have too much respect for the extensive training their minister has received to pit their preferences against his in a contest of wills. People responsible for the finances of the church see it as their privilege to undergird the program administered by their minister, not to determine it, and teachers and counselors see their work as complementing what the minister does rather than competing with it.

Meanwhile, the minister, eager to have the best for his church, seeks to find laymen who excel in fields other than his and turns to them for counsel and assistance. "How we laymen glow with pride," exclaimed one of my laymen, "when our advice or cooperation is sought by 'our' minister!" And he added, "Laymen lose interest if used only as a 'rubber stamp.'" Both laymen and ministers have a very special role to play in the life of the church. Each should play his own role with confidence and each should respect the role of the other. Robert Rodenmayer describes the ideal interplay of lay and ministerial activity when he writes:

> People enjoy doing the things they do well and we all need to be needed. If a room is to be painted or if the church basement might be reconditioned for a better use, willing hands can usually be found. We spend less imagination in other areas. A banker in the parish may be just the person to talk to the young married group about family budgets. Well-instructed lay people can be effective in giving baptismal instruction. Physicians have expert knowledge to contribute. A help both to me and to my people was a woman whose son was among the first to be killed in action in the Second World War. She was a Christian and absorbed her loss like a Christian, quietly and realistically and in the faith. I used to take her with me when I went to call on the families of the other young men we lost and to leave her there for awhile when I had gone. The people could say to me—or think it—that I had not lost my son, but they could not say that to her. It takes various interests and offerings to make a full life in a parish family.[2]

[2] *We Have This Ministry* (New York: Harper & Row, 1959), pp. 60–61.

This kind of cooperative endeavor is the proper relationship between laymen and ministers. It is found among laymen who, in relation to their ministers, are not idolaters, or patrons, or critics, or enemies, or competitors, but coworkers in a great venture, friends in a noble enterprise, disciples of one Master.

In such relationships the ministry becomes a shared endeavor participated in by ministers and laymen alike. Each ministers to the other and both minister to the world. Many laymen, like the one in Evanston in the story with which this chapter began, are ready to tell how some minister led them to a new awareness of God's love. In the best lay-ministerial relationships, laymen bring similar inspiration to their ministers.

It was so in the experience of a friend of mine who had hurried to the side of a layman whose married son had been critically injured. There was a chance he would die before morning. If he lived, it was almost certain he would be a cripple for the rest of his days. His injury, a knife wound in his back, had been inflicted by his young wife, who, in sudden rage, had grabbed the only weapon handy, sinking it to deadly depths. As soon as the seriousness of his injury was recognized by the local doctor, the young husband was flown from his desert home to a large city where he could have the attention of specialists at a leading hospital. His father met him there, but his panic-stricken wife remained at home.

It was while the minister was with the wounded man's father that the grieving parent put through a long-distance telephone call to his daughter-in-law. "Hi, honey," the preacher heard him say with warm reassurance. Then there was a pause as the girl at the other end of the line struggled to hold her emotions under control, and the father added, "That's all right. You don't have to be in control of your voice to talk to us. You know we love you." The minister testifies that in those moments it was as though the forgiving love of God filled the room and traveled over the wires across the miles that separated them, to embrace a frightened, remorseful girl. It touched the heart of the minister as well. How deep the friendship must have grown that night between one minister and one layman. To be related to people at the point where their faith touches the raw wounds and open graves of their existence is to be where real friendships are made. It is to be where ministry happens whether the inspiration travels from clergy to layman or from layman to clergy.

XI

The Churchman at Home

The church does not exist for its own sake. It has a mission to accomplish, a mission to the whole world. The world is large and there are many places to begin the mission as we shall see in the next chapter, but one is more obvious than the rest. That is the home. The church's most direct access to the world is by way of the homes of its members.

There is a sense in which Christianity may be compared with a university in which the church is the lecture hall and the home is the laboratory. What is learned in the lecture hall must be applied in the laboratory or it is of little use; what is done in the laboratory must follow the instruction from the lecture hall or the experiment comes out wrong. The churchman at home is the student in his laboratory. In this chapter we are going to talk about some of the assignments the church gives the student.

The first is to make his home identifiable as Christian.

One way to do this is through the use of religious symbols and ceremonies. Generally speaking, Jews and Catholics make better use of these aids to the development of religious values among members of the family than do Protestants. Much Jewish ceremony centers in the home; Catholic families display the crucifix and a variety of religious pictures.

Protestants, however, shy away from this sort of thing. They shun anything resembling idols or shrines, and they have a marked distaste for display of piety. In part this instinct is sound. Crudely decorated religious mottoes and unartistic sacred art suggest bad taste rather than good religion. But bad religious art has a better alternative than no religious art and that is good religious art. Displaying piety has a better alternative than concealing piety, and that is expressing piety. A home should express the interests and the values of the people in it. A Christian home should express Christian values.

A good beginning is to dedicate one's home with a religious ceremony. The Eisenhowers did that. After they had completed the remodeling of their Gettysburg home, they invited their minister to officiate at an informal family service of dedication. Explaining to him that they had both been raised in homes where people prayed and read the Bible, they asked him to officiate at a simple ceremony to dedicate this, the only home of their own that they had ever had. It was the right thing for a Protestant family to do.

Home dedications are not common, however, and I suspect that most Protestant laymen have never heard of them. Although some denominational books of worship include formal services designed for this purpose, the idea has never caught on with a majority of churchmen. I wish it would. The formal dedication of a new home can remind the members of a family that their home is a sacred trust. It commits them to noble living.

In addition to a service such as this, grace at table and

other practices familiar to churchmen mark the family as Christian. Carefully selected pieces of Christian art or symbols such as a cross or the descending dove representing the presence of the Holy Spirit can be meaningful. Some families use the ancient symbol of the fish as a door marker. Religious albums in the record library, religious books on the reading table, and religious periodicals arriving in the mail all bear witness to the family's central Christian loyalty. Not all of these suggestions will appeal to every churchman. There is no reason why they should. However, every church family should have *some* reminders of its Christian connections. Certainly it would be hard to take the religious commitment of a family seriously if a stranger could enter the home, stay a few hours, and leave without getting a clear indication of its religious flavor.

Another distinguishing mark of the Protestant home is evident participation in the life of the church. Any neighbors who have occasion to observe should have no difficulty in identifying well-established habits of church attendance. One family I know has a simple rule to guarantee faithfulness in church attendance. I learned of it quite by accident one Sunday afternoon when I called the father to see if he would like to attend a meeting I thought would interest him. "I can't leave the property," he said. A bit mystified, I repeated, "You can't leave the property? What do you mean?" "We have a custom in our family," he answered, "that anyone who doesn't get to church Sunday morning can't leave the home base during the day. I overslept this morning and didn't get to church, so I'm grounded."

No doubt the rule was established as an aid to getting the children off to church each Sunday with a minimum of complaint. But whoever the rule was designed to serve, it applied equally to all and became a unique reminder to each that for this family, church attendance was important. Individual family traditions of this kind are wholesome and add the unique stamp of the particular family to the religious commitment they share with many others.

But while symbols, ceremonies, and customs are important, the family wishing to establish them should be aware of certain hazards. For one thing, overpious churchmen can work too hard at it and emerge with a religiosity that is a strain to live with. Religious language sometimes hides a bitter spirit, and religious customs can harden into instruments of autocratic power. I once knew a man who used the family prayer as a device for domination. Life is so sensitively balanced that every virtue harbors its own threat and every achievement is next door to failure. Devotional practices are easily corrupted. That's why I add to the suggestion of religious ceremonies in the home the warning that it can be overdone. I want my family to be religious but I don't want to impose any exaggerated piety upon them. They deserve something better.

What they deserve is a home in which each member of the family is free to expose the existence of his worst self while being nourished and supported in the development of his best self. They need the atmosphere of robust honesty and glad commitment. But they need to know these blessings come at a price and that all of them have to work at it if they are to maintain a Christian home. There will be difficulties, of course, but whether they face big problems, such as active opposition, or nuisance problems, such as the last-minute Sunday morning congestion at the bathroom door, they should know that every difficulty is minor compared with the privilege of churchmanship. Rejoicing in Christian discipleship, let them drink whatever cup of inconvenience is served to them, and be thankful.

Let them rejoice also in being known as a Christian family. They are so identified not only through church attendance and the symbols and ceremonies in their home, but likewise through the habitual behavior of each family member. Anyone encountering a person who seemingly by instinct practices honesty, humility, kindness, forgiveness, understanding, and purposive discipline, should be able to guess that he has been nourished in the Christian tradition. These characteristics may be found elsewhere to be sure, especially in persons who are loyal to other great religions. Nevertheless, they remain important to the Christian home and clearly mark the members of the Christian family. If God in Christ is the central loyalty around which a family is oriented, this fact will show.

And how can a home resist the pull toward its natural center which is the God who "set the solitary in families" —and "who, when he appeared on earth," as *Christian Century* editor Kyle Haselden reminds us, "came not from the sky but into a family . . . [and] who crowned the home prior to the church and state."

A few years ago a boy named Albert Kogler was fatally injured by a shark in the waters of San Francisco Bay. He lived for a little while after he was pulled from the water, and his last words were, "I love God and I love my mother and I love my father. O God, help me, God help me." It is a grand thing when children thus link together the names of their parents and of their God.

This gives the motive power for the second assignment for the churchman in his laboratory. *He should love-condition the home.* Christianity involves the practice of many virtues, none of which should be neglected. Yet, as Paul reminds us, love is of special importance. It creates the climate in which the others can be properly nourished.

Love is aggressive goodwill. To love others is to serve them, to seek their happiness, to build their self-confidence. It is to nourish their strengths and help them to face their weaknesses. Love is a conviction about the nature of reality, a commitment to a way of life. To love another is to acknowledge his worth in the sight of God; it is to accept an appropriate measure of responsibility for his welfare; it is to seek his company and to rejoice in his success. One who loves gives freely, without asking that anything be given in return. He accepts responsibility for his own sin, without pointing out the sin of others. Recognizing the inadequacies of those he loves, he accentuates their virtues; acknowledging their failures, he remembers their successes.

His love is continuous: it is never interrupted while he decides whether or not it is deserved. His love is patient: it never grows weary when results are not evident. His love is endless: it is never suspended as a threat of ultimate withdrawal. One who loves is always confident, but never arrogant; secure in the certainty that love is of God, he is humble in the knowledge that he has not yet loved enough.

When practiced in a normal home, love generally catches on. Family members grow confident in it, and find courage to practice it beyond the family circle. Armed with love, they are better prepared for life. This fact has now been scientifically tested, and there is no longer any doubt that children deprived of love lose the incentive for living, children raised on snatches of uncertain love lose their sense of security, and children nourished in the strong love of a truly Christian home possess inner resources that the unloved can scarcely imagine. Nurtured in the methods of love at home, adults are prepared to handle routine employment without growing dull, tense business pressures without caving in, and declining professional effectiveness without losing hope. Such is the miracle performed by the home that is love-conditioned by the Christian laymen who live in it.

Yet, important as love is, it remains a mystery to many. Three misconceptions in particular cause difficulty.

The first is the tendency to equate love with sexual passion. Physical attraction is an important part of married love, but it is not the whole of it. It is the inflated part of it. Sometimes it grows so big that other considerations are completely overlooked. That accounts for the more than occasional young couple who, unsuited for one another and unprepared for family responsibilities, disregard all laws of common sense and get married simply because they are "in love."

They are using the wrong term. It would clarify things if there were a good term available but there is not. "Infatuation" doesn't say it. Neither does "lust." Whatever word one uses, the important fact to know is that physical attraction is not the all-sufficient ingredient for love, and taken by itself may be intensely selfish. This is the opposite of love.

This misunderstanding about love's meaning is a time bomb. Sooner or later it blows up the home that harbors it. Its destructive power is in its inevitable logic, which runs like this: Love is a physical feeling. It is the basis for marriage. In happy marriage the feeling continues unabated. In less fortunate situations the feeling subsides after the wedding. Without the feeling there is no love. Without the love the marriage is dead. Dead things are to be buried. For the sake of appearances and for the reassurance of relatives, a counselor may be called on to administer artificial respiration, but if the marriage fails to respond, a funeral is held in the courtroom where the judge eulogizes marriage in general and commits this particular marriage to an uneasy resting place. Meanwhile lawyers make arrangements for the proper disposition of the estate of the deceased. Acknowledged as untimely, the death of the marriage is not seriously mourned. It is left behind with few regrets but with hopes for better luck next time.

Many people hold this misconception about the meaning of love. The result is a growing mountain of misery as more and more homes are thoughtlessly established and unnecessarily broken. Or holding the marriage together for whatever reasons they may have decided upon, too many couples conclude that the fire of love has burned out and they have no choice but to live on in the drab atmosphere of lovelessness.

The second misconception about love is that either you have it or you don't have it. If you don't have it you can't express it; if you do have it you can't help expressing it.

It is one of the sentimental heresies of our time that it is dishonest to express loving emotions unless they are felt. This error comes in the same package with that other heresy that negative emotions *must* be expressed because they *are* felt. Almost no one seems to be saying that loving goodwill is to be expressed at all times because it is the right way to live whether one feels like it or not. It is precisely at the point where kindness comes hard that it becomes a virtue. It is at the exact moment when one is tempted toward disloyalty that loyalty has meaning. That is why Frederick Speakman says:

> . . . even in marriage, love is *not* primarily something you feel! *Love is something you do!*
>
> It would make the marriage vow a farce to imagine it means any two mortals can stand before God and solemnly promise he and she will feel tender and loving toward each other every moment till death does them part! For emotions come and go, and tenderness has its highs and lows, but the heart of Christian marriage is that one is able to vow thus before God: "I will act toward this person in a way that I will act toward no one else from now on, no matter what the climate or the season of my feelings. This love will find its measure in me in the things I *do*."[1]

In Christian marriage there are vows to be lived by. A promise has been made and it must be kept. Swiss theologian Emil Brunner goes so far as to say, "Fidelity is the mark of marriage, not love, not romance, not harmony, not peace, but fidelity and promise." Agreeing with his emphasis, I should prefer to state it a little differently, perhaps like this: "Love is the mark of marriage, not romance, not harmony, not peace, but love, which means fidelity, promise and unfailing goodwill."

The third misconception about love is the notion that it is the absence of conflict. I am tempted to embrace this heresy myself. With a strong distaste for unpleasantness, I sometimes try to stop the arguments of my children by

[1] *Love Is Something You Do* (Westwood, N.J.: Fleming H. Revell Company, 1959), pp. 16–17.

telling them to "be sweet" or to "keep it light." One day when I offered such counsel, one of my sons, far from simmering down, turned his anger on me. "Oh, Dad," he said, 'it makes me so mad when you say that!" Without realizing it, I was denying the children their normal outlet for feelings of hostility. A Christian home is not a place where anger is never expressed. It is a fellowship in which hostile feelings are acknowledged and siphoned off in ways that are not harmful to others. The parent who will never allow his child to raise his voice or give vent to destructive feelings may be raising a model child, but a disturbed adult. He may be keeping peace, but he is not expressing love.

That is not to say that a Christian home should allow unrestrained expression of feelings. Such freedom to externalize the negative produces rude, irresponsible people, and there are already too many of those around. One wishes that their parents had taught them a long while ago that open displays of anger are not acceptable methods of making a point. Outbursts of temper, like undressing in public, constitute indecent exposure and should be met by a Christian gentleman by turning his head away to give the offender time to cover the nakedness of his emotions. No Christian home should countenance temper tantrums, vitriolic attacks, or destructive expressions of anger. It should teach children, from the time they are very young, that these are not acceptable ways of handling the tensions of living. There should be no hesitancy in branding them as taboo.

On the other hand, the Christian home is not free from conflicts. In fact, if there is no conflict, the home is not Christian. Suppose that I have laid down restrictions within which my children are to live; I have given orders for things they are to do; and I have scolded them for their infractions of the rules. If they come to feel resentful of what I have done—and they will—there had better be room in the circle of our family love for them to challenge me. Out of the conflict of their will against mine, there should emerge a better plan, greater understanding, and deeper affection. Frank acknowledgment of irritating behavior is not the failure of love, but an expression of it. Family life without conflict may be peaceful coexistence, but it is not creative love in action. To assume that if people love each other there is no conflict is to misread the meaning of love. To have no fear of conflict, knowing that love will harness dissension's violent energies to some good cause, is to understand the fullness of love.

The task of the Christian layman, therefore, is not to eliminate conflict in the home, but to nourish the love that can control and direct it. Rachel Henderlite's family must have accomplished this, for she dedicated her book, *A Call to Faith*, "To My Family—father, mother, sister, brother—who, by living together as a Christian family and arguing heatedly about theology around the dinner table, have given me my faith."

We learn love by loving, and we love when we extend a kindness to another, put his welfare above our own, show a genuine interest in who he is and what he does, express a spirit of joy for his sake if not for our own, care for him when he is sick, guide him when he is lost or confused, support him when he is testing his own ability, and believe in him when he has come to doubt himself. All this and much more is what it means to love. It means to have the mind of Christ in us. It is what the Christian layman works hardest on in that laboratory that is his home.

His third laboratory assignment is to *acknowledge individuality*. The Christian home should accentuate the uniqueness of each member of the family.

It should encourage a wife and mother to be everything the words "wife" and "mother" imply, and to be herself, as a very special wife and mother besides. She can attain this integrity of selfhood only in the context of a family in which it is expected of her.

She, more than any other member of the household, personifies all that is meant by home. She is its heart and its busy fingers. Because love comes more naturally to her, than to the others, her responsibility to be loving is greater. She is the teacher in the art of it. Others learn it from her example.

In his report on a visit with Albert Schweitzer, Norman Cousins describes the African families that cluster about the hospital at Lamboréné and assist in the care of their loved ones under treatment there. Depicting the universality of mother love and the wonder of human sacrifice in its most elemental expressions and primitive settings, he describes the women cooking over homemade stoves just outside the patient's rooms or the small cubicles in the open wards. "I noticed one woman squatting close to an improvised stove consisting of a large pit in which she was making a banana milk stew for her family," he writes. "The milk was her own. She deftly worked each breast close to the pan, sending streams of her milk into the stew. Here was the eternal woman in the oldest drama in the world—giving her totality to the cause of life near her, infinitely resourceful, inventive, responsible. The banana milk stew sent up its steam and the woman sang softly."

That is motherhood. Lovingly giving of herself, the mother sings, adding the inspiration of something spiritual to the basic requirements of the physical survival of her family.

It was spontaneous acknowledgment of this virtue of motherhood that once drew an exclamation of relief and pride from my youngest son. He was riding in the back seat of our car, accompanying my wife and me on some routine trip about town, when we came to a busy intersection. Suddenly I saw a woman who had fallen face down in the crosswalk. She was directly in front of a line of cars poised like runners waiting for the signal to begin a race. Yet no one made a move to help, although she was in plain view and was obviously unable to regain her footing without aid. Quickly I stopped my car beside her, hoping to block any other car whose driver with eyes for nothing but the signal might fail to see her. Before the car was stopped, my wife was on the street helping the fallen pedestrian to her feet and to her intended destination across the boulevard. Tommy watched in awed silence until the critical moments had passed. Then relaxing, he smiled broadly and said, "Good old Mom!" I agreed. How spontaneously and inevitably the Christian mother teaches the lessons of love.

But what of the Christian father? While the role of the mother is well established, the responsibility of the father remains vague. His "image," once very clear, has been tarnished. In the Christian tradition "father" is a great word. The strong feeling of it is expressed in the hymn, "Faith of Our Fathers." The ancient Jew traced his lineage through his father, and the most important thing about him was whose son he was. The great men in history are referred to as the nations' "fathers." And "Father" was used as an honorary title for those most deeply loved and respected. A father's crowning honor, however, is that Jesus called God, "Father."

Even in the recent American past, the word "father" had the ring of the woodsman's axe about it. Known as "the head of the house," the old-time father set the rules, paid the bills, administered discipline, and saw that justice was done. No doubt he was too autocratic at times, but he was a *man!*—conscious of his position of authority and determined to use it for the good of all.

But today father appears less noble. Grace and Fred Hechinger, *New York Times* writers, describe the typical "movie" father as a "child-man," "the male boob," the member of the family who loudly objects to what his children are doing but meekly surrenders and pays the bills when mother, interceding in behalf of the children, brings him up to date on modern youth. Comic strip fathers, like Dagwood, or "Fred" in the Flintstones fit the image. They are like children trying to play a man's role—lovable blunderbusses easily manipulated by the other members of the family.

One reason for this change in the father role is the

misapplication of democracy to family life. There has been too much sentimental talk about family councils and democratic decisions arrived at jointly between parents and children. One can agree that children are persons whose ideas should be listened to, whose feelings should be appreciated, and whose rights should be respected, without buying the idea that the family is a democracy or should be operated as one. The democratic concept that all men are created equal does not mean that all members of a family have equal rights, equal responsibility, equal needs, equally sound judgment, or equal authority. We are experiencing a crisis in the American home today precisely because we have encouraged this assumption. Afraid of being undemocratic in the home (where the principle of love, not the principle of democracy, should be the guiding rule), many fathers have surrendered their responsibility as head of the house just because they were outvoted. This growing paternal timidity shows up on personality tests which indicate that women are becoming more aggressive and men more submissive.

This trend should be reversed, and Christian fathers should be the first to regain their self-confidence. They should know that extreme permissiveness never was a manly stance and now, fortunately, is considered old-fashioned. Today it is proper and respectable to lay down rules and enforce them. The more advanced youth want their dads to "stop trying to be nice guys" and be fathers. One man saw the light the day he acknowledged the simple fact that his "son has lots of pals his own age, but he only has one father."

The Christian father must regain his courage to be strong. Standing tall, he must reclaim his position as head of the house. Once again he must become a legitimate hero to his sons and daughters, setting them an example and holding before them the noblest Christian ideals.

Unfortunately, today's typical father is slow to accept that challenge. Instead of teaching his children to do what is right, he defends his children in doing wrong. Uncooperative parents are one of the juvenile officers' most serious problems.

Instead of setting his children an example, he follows the example of his children. One writer declares that "adults not only condone but adopt the teen-age culture."

Instead of inspiring his children with high ideals, he kills the ideals of his children. Many fathers discourage their sons and daughters from going into the most humanitarian vocations. This is because they are more interested in their children's affluence than in their Christian influence; more eager for them to be financially and socially "secure" than spiritually and intellectually significant.

The world needs a new crop of idealistic fathers. This is more important than one might think, because "father" is more than a person. "Father" is a symbol. He is a symbol of religion; a priest is called "Father." He is the symbol of patriotism; we refer to our country as our "Fatherland." He is the symbol of love and truth and the whole creative process of the universe; God is our Father!

In this age when so many men disregard religion, show scant respect for government and law, and dismiss God along with Santa Claus, there is a need for fathers who are living symbols of everything that's good.

Children, also, are symbols of the highest human qualities. That is one thing that has placed them in such an honored position in Christian homes. Jesus said they were like heaven itself, and that adults should strive to be like them.

Nevertheless, as any parent can testify, they are not angels. They can be quite difficult. That's our problem. Because children exact a heavy toll of nervous energy from the adults in the household, it is easy to fall into a negative attitude about them and with them. To a certain extent this is inevitable, and parents should not punish themselves with remorse for showing impatience or being more cross than the children's behavior warrants. There is some comfort in the assurance that children can take a great deal of this without suffering permanent damage as long as they have no reason to doubt their parents' love. There is also reassurance in the idea that children need to encounter the real world of undeserved harshness while they are young, so as to learn to deal with it when they are older. They might as well find out early that parents have feelings.

Still, the Christian layman will take his parental responsibility seriously and do all he can to nurture the growth of great character in his children. He will do this "in every way, by precept and example," as he promises when each child is baptized. He will also do it through loving encouragement. As I look back on the younger years of my own children and my observations of the homes of others, one fact falls in central focus: aside from the obvious mistakes of parental immorality and irresponsibility, the extremes of authoritarianism and permissiveness, or the erratic alternation between strictness and laxity, nothing is harder on children than too much criticism and too little praise.

Oddly, Christian parents are more prone to make this mistake than others. They want so much to perfect their children that they fall into the habit of criticizing everything they do. They seldom stop to think that when we criticize others, we are saying in effect, "I do not love you the way you are. If you want my love, you must change your behavior." Criticized children feel unworthy, and defeated. They come to believe that they cannot be loved unless they are perfect, and knowing how imperfect they are, they begin to doubt that anyone loves them.

Christian laymen should praise their children not only because it is a fine way to be a good parent, but also because of their own childlikeness. For in the last analysis, we are all children. That's what Jesus said the disciples were, and John often referred to the early Christians as "children." Something he wrote in one of his letters should have meaning for every layman: "See what love the Father has given us, that we should be called children of God; and so we are" (I John 3:1). Thus as the churchman accentuates the individuality of each member of the family, he finds also the bond that makes them one, for "now are we the sons of God" (I John 3:2).

The fourth assignment for the Christian layman is to *find more ways to use the laboratory in cooperation with the lecture hall.* Or, to put it directly, to *make his home an outpost of the church.* The early church often met in the homes of the Christians. Many churches have been organized at a meeting in someone's living room or around their kitchen table.

The homes of some laymen in the community in which I grew up seemed inseparable from the church. We had one Sunday-school teacher who taught us the Christian faith in the cubicle that was our classroom on Sunday morning and on his farm on Sunday afternoon. Our friends' parents often invited us to hold our committee meetings in their homes, where we experienced the warm goodness of devout families. Not infrequently the gang came to our house, and, while we were not prepared to entertain them as stylishly as others, we were generous with the happy enthusiasm of a large family whose life was oriented to the church.

Many laymen never think of using their homes in behalf of the church. The church is something they go to, not something they bring home. They fail to see their own livingroom, den, or kitchen as a proper place for activities normally associated with a church building.

But other laymen see it differently. A friend of ours once wrote us a letter in which she said that the church has always seemed like home to the members of her family. She added:

> This feeling of at-homeness in the church had its counterpart in our feeling of at-churchness in our home. Religion seemed a natural part of our daily living. Our concerns and activities of home and church were so intermingled that there was a vital continuity be-

tween the two. It seemed natural to pray together. We had our regular family worship at the breakfast table, but there were also those spontaneous moments of prayer and worship which make such precious memories. I remember so well, for instance, the early morning call which told of the death of my husband's father. It was the first such loss that the children had been old enough to share, and it was plain to see that their young hearts had felt the wrench which only death can give. I was so thankful at that moment for a husband for whom it was natural to pray. He thanked God for such a good father and asked that we might all be worthy of having been inspired by his devoted life. As he prayed that we might be strong for the experiences which lay ahead in the next few days, I'm sure that our daughters felt that God was sharing our grief rather than having taken their grandfather away from them.

A true Christian home is an outpost of the church. In a real sense it *is* the church in the neighborhood where it is located and with the people who are fortunate enough to come into it.

This brings us to the final laboratory assignment I am suggesting for the Christian layman. It is different from the others, but it involves the same emphasis on the home. *The layman should accentuate the uniqueness of his minister's residence.*

A parsonage is something special. It is a "second home" for anyone who needs such a haven. Robert Rodenmayer expresses it when he says that "there should be at least one house in every community to which people can go for no reason at all. They do not even have to have a problem! And what more appropriate home could there be than that of the man who ministers in the name of Christ?"

Bishop Herbert Welch, now long past his hundredth

birthday, holds a similar attitude. Speaking of his days in the local pastorate, he writes, "Our home became a second home to students, schoolteachers, fraternity brothers, and in our back parlor even some courting was done. The ministry of the parsonage was no less important than the ministry of the pulpit."

A parsonage is an available home. It is a place where youth groups can meet in the atmosphere of a Christian family and come to know how the minister looks in an apron, how his wife handles a busy household, and how they both relate to their children. Designed to meet human need in a direct and personal way, it is a place of caring, hoping, dreaming, planning.

The parsonage has played an important role in my own ministry. It shares almost equally with the pulpit in the memories it brings to mind of lives changed, sorrows softened, careers determined, and hopes restored. "My decision to enter the ministry was made as I talked with you one night in your living room," a minister said to me one day. He had been in our church during his student days. On another occasion, a happy housewife, mother of three fine children, said, "I have never told you this before, but I would never have married if I had not lived in your home the year I finished my nurse's training. It was there that I learned for the first time that marriage could be happy."

People want an example. It isn't enough to read about how to maintain a happy home. They need to see one in action. And they should have the opportunity to do so. The only intimate glimpse some people have of what goes on inside other people's homes is provided by the gossip columns and movie magazines that feature patterns of domestic devastation. To counteract these "examples" of what home life is like, something positive is needed. There is a deep but seldom recognized human need in every community for some home that can be pointed to with pride, and the reassurance that the highest standards of home life are both desirable and possible. The parsonage should be that incarnate hope. It should stand as a symbol of quality and a reminder that a Christ-centered home is a happy home.

Some will reject this concept of the parsonage. A minister's family needs privacy as much as anyone else, they argue. As far as they are concerned, this kind of fish-bowl existence is strictly for the fish. Besides, no one should be forced to be public examples of private living.

These objections are important. Any tendency to shift the focus of the ministry from one who is God's servant to one who is man's example is cause for alarm. So is any further infringement on family privacy in a society bent on exposing every secret.

But the objections miss the point. To accentuate the importance of the parsonage, rather than to let it melt into the community like some numberless house in a housing tract, is not to shatter privacy but to fulfill ministry. It is like topping the church with a steeple to rise above the buildings around it. The purpose is not to elevate a building but to lift up an ideal. And the purpose of accentuating the importance of the parsonage is not to put the parsonage family on parade, but to symbolize the central importance of Christian home life.

Besides, the matter is not entirely one of choice. The minister's family, because of their publicly recognized commitment to a way of life that is said to be ideal, *are* on exhibition, whether they wish to be or not. It is the way of life the minister chose when he accepted his call to the ministry and the kind of home his wife agreed to when she accepted his invitation to join the team. Their only choice is whether to accept with grace and dignity the responsibility that is theirs, or to run from duty and seek escape from the life they have chosen. The conscientious Protestant minister along with his family and church seek to be Christian in everything they do, and they should welcome in Christian humility each opportunity to witness to the Lordship of Christ in every act of their lives.

They need the layman's support in this. If their home is to symbolize the best in family life, the church should provide the kind of house that encourages it. If their door is to be open to the world, no layman should think he is pampering the clergy by including the costs of parsonage maintenance, yard work, and household help in the church budget, along with similar provisions for the church building itself. If the minister's wife is to resist the temptation to be gainfully employed to help meet the costs of a growing family and serve full time in parsonage and church, thoughtful laymen may want to make a study of her actual "professional expenses" in work for which she receives no salary. Discovering the cost, they will surely share it.

While recognizing the uniqueness of the minister's home and the extra attention required to keep it "special"—not for benefit of clergy, but for the sake of the church and the gospel it proclaims—the Christian layman will remember not only the Sabbath day, but also the home, to keep it holy. And he will not forget the sense in which every layman is a minister, and every church home a parsonage.

XII

Ambassadors of Faith

The church can overemphasize the home. In fact, it has been overemphasizing it for the past twenty or thirty years. How much improvement this has brought to family life among Christians is hard to say. But it can be said with reasonable certainty that it has had a paralyzing effect upon the church and its mission.

To make this assertion is not to detract from anything that was said in the preceding chapter. Christian homes are fundamental, and the church should nourish them. But this fact does not justify the rash of family-centered churches, family camps, parents' nights, mothers' days, children's programs, family weeks, families of the year, and all those other programs, emphases, and materials presented to the church with a characteristic "now-this-is-for-everybody" smile of self-satisfaction. Gibson Winter, author of *The Suburban Captivity of the Churches,* describes the suburban minister as "a supplement to the didie service," who, along with his entire congregation, is compelled to subordinate the deep meaning of the Christian faith "to the middle-class preoccupation with children."

Considering the prominence of family imagery in the Christian religion, it is not surprising that the home should be emphasized by the church. We speak of Mary, Joseph, and Jesus as "the Holy Family." We call God "Father" and look to heaven as our home. This does not trouble me. Our family imagery is good, as is our enthusiasm for creating Christian homes among our members. The disturbing thing is the extent to which the church has been captured by the home. Nothing could serve the purposes of evil more effectively than to trap the church in domesticity.

God calls us to take the message of Christ to the world. We answer His call and go—home! Home to our comfortable middle-class neighborhood, home to our newspaper and dishwasher, home to the satisfaction that in spite of the annoyances incorporated within it, the Christian family is something very much like the Kingdom of God. The home should be the bridge from the church to the world. Too often we have made it the church's final resting place. If the churchman carries the church beyond his home at all, it is likely to be only as far as the homes of nonmembers whom he calls "good prospects." These are people whose family patterns are so much like his own that they would "fit in" his church as naturally as the new baby fits into the family that has been expecting it.

This limits his contacts because most people aren't at home much anymore. They spend most of their time elsewhere, and in other relationships than the family. They are at school, in offices, and in shops. They are on the road or in the air. They are loitering on street corners, sitting in taverns, meeting with clients, recuperating in hospitals, and living behind prison walls, resenting society. Some are in Vietnam, some are fanning the flames of a smoldering Watts, and some are trying to cooperate with the computers in making sense of the latest election results, packed as they are with subtle inferences about white backlash and other manifestations of a rapidly changing society. They are doing all sorts of things besides sitting around the family table, bowing their heads for the blessing. The church should be with them. The Christian faith should get to them. That's the challenge with which this chapter deals: the church's mission to the world.

To understand it properly we must back up and get a running start. We must know the logic that leads us out where it is hard to go, or we shall never get there. This is the way it runs:

We are Christians: men and women committed to Jesus Christ.

We are churchmen: Christians united in obedience to Christ.

We are laymen and ministers: churchmen assigned to specific areas of responsibility in doing the work of Christ.

In one sense the job is the same for all of us. We are full-time Christians seeking to do God's will in all things. In another sense, our jobs are different. The work of the ministers is largely in the church and with committed Christians; the work of the laymen is largely outside the church and with "non" or nominal Christians. Clergymen bring the ministries of Christ to the laymen. Laymen bring the ministries of Christ to the world. Here are some of the ways different people have expressed this idea.

The clergy are the commissioned officers; the laity are the troops.

The clergy are the conductors of a symphony; the laity produce the music.

The clergy are the coaches; the laity are the team members.

The clergy are the servants, washing dusty feet; the laity are the saints whose feet grow dusty on the paths of the secular world.

The clergy are the mechanics who keep the cars running; the laity are the drivers who cover the road.

You will quickly see that none of these descriptions is totally adequate, but you will also see the truth that runs through all of them: that ministry means mediating Christ to the world and that it is the task of the total church. Within this task there is a normal and necessary division of responsibility by which field work falls largely to laymen, while the clergy train them for the task and inspire them in it.

The field work is described in different ways. The job is *witness:* to tell the people who Christ is and what he has done for us. The job is *evangelism:* to offer a lost generation the One who can save it. The job is *mission:* to settle in a secular environment, allowing oneself to be absorbed by it as leaven is absorbed by dough, so that the spirit of Christ may permeate the whole. The job is *service:* to give, to teach, to heal, to comfort, to encourage, and to put a strong shoulder under the other fellow's load. The job is *ministry,* which is the word we use to summarize the total task.

This concept is the thesis of many books that have appeared in the last ten or fifteen years. George W. Webber defines the church as *God's Colony in Man's World,* and speaks of *The Congregation in Mission.* Langdon Gilkey faces the problem of *How the Church Can Minister to the World Without Losing Itself.* Howard Grimes notes the new awareness of the distinctive responsibility of laymen for the total ministry of the church in what he defines as *The Rebirth of the Laity.* Charles W. Ranson suggests that the church exists *That the World May Know* and Elton Trueblood calls us *The Company of the Committed.* Each of these books, along with a sudden flood of others focusing on the laymen, has a distinctive contribution to make, but the conviction that the work of the Christian layman is more outside the organized church than in it seems to be common to all of them. Together they constitute a call to the church to recover its central mission, which is not to please itself, but to win a world.

This idea is not new, but renewed. Jesus said, "As the Father has sent me, even so I send you" (John 20:21), and "Go therefore and make disciples of all nations . . ." (Matt. 28:19). Speaking of Christ's "reconciling the world to himself," and then placing that responsibility to the world in our hands by "entrusting to us the message of reconciliation," Paul concludes that ". . . we are ambassadors for Christ . . ." (II Cor. 5:19–20).

Ambassadors are a nation's official representatives abroad. As representatives of the Kingdom of God in human society, Christians are ambassadors of faith. Or, as Paul told the laymen of Corinth, they are letters from Christ, dispatched through the church to a world waiting to receive the mail.

Few have expressed the ambassadorial role of the Christian more effectively than a second-century churchman in his *Letter to Diognetus*. After pointing out that Christians are free from eccentricities that make them oddities in the world to which they are sent and that they speak the same language, eat the same food, wear the same clothing, and follow the same customs as the people among whom they live, he notes that they are simultaneously citizens and aliens. "They have a share in everything as citizens, and endure everything as foreigners. Every foreign land is their father land, and yet for them every father land is a foreign land . . .

"They busy themselves on earth, but their citizenship is in heaven . . .

"To put it simply: What the soul is in the body, the Christians are in the world."

As an ambassador, each layman has his specific assignment. Assignments will vary according to needs and the ability to meet them. In some cases the decision as to where a person is to represent the faith is automatic. For example, no one needs to tell a Christian mother that she is an ambassador of Christ to her family. This is the "country" to which she is sent. She may be given other responsibilities as well, but there is no retreat from her primary commission to be a letter from Christ to her own children. The same is true of a man or woman in a given vocation. Since his vocation is the "foreign land" in which he spends much of his time, no one should have to tell him that he is God's representative in that environment.

Another group of ambassadorial assignments comes directly from Christ to the individual. No one can predict or chart these, and they are hard to evaluate. But faith in their existence is an important part of our Protestant heritage. Our belief that God speaks to the individual conscience with commands that supersede all human directives is the keystone in our defense of freedom, our trust in democracy, and our declaration of human rights. Individualism at its best is rooted in the assurance that God relates uniquely to each of us as separate persons. Thus Christ puts a concern for racial justice in the heart of one, a determination to do something about juvenile crime in the mind of another, and a compassion for alcoholics, dope addicts, or unwed mothers in the soul of a third. This direct action of the Spirit of God within him may be a layman's most authentic ambassadorial appointment.

In addition to the assignments that are automatic and the ones that come from the direct communication of God's Spirit with the Christian, there is another group that is made directly by the church. As this fellowship of committed Christians sees the world as a whole, it locates crucial areas where the most skilled ambassadors are needed. Denominational, interdenominational, and interfaith commissions on race, international relations, crime, or poverty are made up of churchmen who have responded to the church's call for ambassadors of reconciliation. As the church develops a growing understanding of the role of the layman as ambassador, these "foreign assignments" will no doubt increase in number and significance, and the church's "state department" will replace the "department of the interior" in major importance. The organized church, whose institutionalism is the whipping boy of Christians impatient for progress, will retool its massive machinery in a way that will channel its power toward the accomplishment of the one great task that it has today.

As the church openly acknowledges that membership means discipleship and that every layman must be assigned to an ambassadorial post if the work of the church in the world is to be done, suitable embassies will be established and churchmen placed in them. The best minds of the church, both lay and ministerial, will concentrate on this matter until ways are found to penetrate every segment of human society with the gospel of Jesus Christ. There will be no rude imposing of one's faith upon others, after the manner of religious and political bigots whose doctrines are dogmatic, whose solutions are superficial, and whose manner is arrogant. Neither will the evasion and avoidance of the recent past continue, nailing the cynical and often deserved label of "irrelevant" to the door of the church. Both the crude imposition of sectarian absolutism upon society and the crass indifference of organized religion to the agony of society are chapters of Christian history that are closing. Now, in rethought expressions of our faith, restructured machinery of organization, and renewed committment to Christian discipleship, churchmen are writing the new chapter of redemptive infiltration into the world. That's what the incarnation is all about. This is the revolution we described in Chapter I. It is the renewal so many have prayed for and that is already well on its way.

There will be resistance. Not everyone wants the church renewed. It functions more to their advantage as it came to be during the plush days of the midcentury religious boom. There is no doubt that many laymen prefer a church that spends its time preserving the society it should redeem, adopting standards it should reject or improve, learning from those it should be teaching, invoking the divine blessing on questionable enterprises, stroking guilt feelings instead of uprooting guilt, substituting fellowship for service, opinion for conviction, contributions for dedication, and the assurance of its own comfort for a responsible role in a society that is already too satisfied with itself.

Gibson Winter sees American churches as rallying centers for the preservation of middle-class standards, and says, "The Church is now a reflection of the economic ladder." Like many other observers of the current scene, he sees the religious institutions we have inherited from the recent past as decreasingly religious and increasingly institutional: "In place of the sacraments, we have the committee meeting; in place of confession, the bazaar; in place of pilgrimage, the dull drive to hear the deadly speaker; in place of community, a collection of functions."

Peter L. Berger takes a similar position. He describes the religion found in today's churches as "starry-eyed optimism, a naive credulity in the ideologies of the status quo, something that goes well together with an unthinking if benign conservatism in all areas of life."

Persons committed to the concept of the church so colorfully described by these writers will not welcome the revolution! Some of them will be frightened by it merely because they do not understand it. Some of them will launch a holy crusade to stop it, believing it to be a monstrous evil. More committed to the American middle-class way of life than to the Christian faith, some will drop away when the church becomes more devoted to the latter than to the former. Opposition will be expressed in attacks on the clergy, pressure on church legislative bodies, slashing of financial support and withdrawal of membership.

Because many of those who oppose the revolution are the people who have been footing the church's bills, keeping its buildings in repair, hiring its preachers, and transporting its youth to camp, their resistance cannot be taken lightly. This is why so many of the "revolutionaries" are concluding that it is better to leave the church than to try to reform it. This is a coward's retreat. These people, boasting of boldness, are running in fear. Afraid of failure if they try to win the opposition to their position, they write it off as hopeless and turn away. Afraid of the responsibility that would fall on their shoulders if heavy givers should withdraw their support, they redirect their own resources into what they consider to be more creative channels. Claiming to have a purer concept of the Christian faith than is held by whatever it is they think of when they say "the church," they merely sweep their own inadequacies under the carpet of ecclesiastical snobbery. Their attack on the organized church is timely and important. Their despair of it is cowardly and arrogant. Their criticisms are to be taken seriously, but one can have little respect for their lack of institutional responsibility, their speck-in-the-eye approach to the other fellow's evil, or their weak faith in the power of God to renew even so old and tradition-encrusted an institution as the church.

So let the modern critics of the church review the stance from which they fire their shots. If they are in the church and love it and are ready to suffer with and for it, let them speak. The church must change, and who but clear-eyed prophets speaking in the name of God have ever led the way toward renewal, or ever will? We have had enough of sharp tongues ripping through the church that gave them birth, like delinquents expressing guilt for their betrayal of their mother's love by committing matricide. What conscience has the man who credits the church with having nourished his faith, only to turn and strike it blow on blow and then depart, like one who having milked his benefactor dry, destroys him?

We need reform. But let the reformer reform himself. If he is a prophet let him speak the truth, however hard it is for us to take. And if the church expels him, let him know the consolation of all true prophets of the Lord, the knowledge that he's right, and some day will be vindicated. But if he is only soured on institutions, he is less noble. We can still listen to what he has to say since even accusation couched in anger or in hatred may have its modicum of truth. Let the church evaluate his blows for what they are, the outburst of the child who kicks the steps he stumbles on. The real reformer knows the church has strong men and women in it, schooled in the Christian faith, ready to sacrifice for it, waiting for leadership that is more than hysterical reaction to an institution that bewilders them.

Our task is to steer a course that takes its bearings from the Bible, not from the latest rebel to spurn the church or the reactionary who doesn't want the church to shake because it makes him nervous. Many will not like the course we take. It will be too extreme for some and too conservative for others. This is a fact of life that we must understand and cope with. But we must take our bearings from neither left nor right but from ahead. The mark toward which we press is "the upward call of God in Christ Jesus" (Phil. 3:14).

That call is clearer today than in most periods of church history. It is this: *The church must now send its "ambassadors" into the hot spots of society.* Our mission is to the total culture. This seems to me to be the strong clear voice of providence, confirmed by consistency with the gospel's demands, relevancy to the world's needs, and the emergence of leaders with both the ability and vision to lead us toward that goal. It is the new thrust into which the church must pour its strength.

That is not to say that previous generations of Christians were not called to this same task. Taking the gospel to the whole world has always been the mission of the church. Yet today the call is different. For the disciples, "the whole world" meant mostly the gentiles. For the Roman Church, it meant the barbarians to the north. To nineteenth-century Christians it meant the Orient and the "heathen tribes" of the "dark continent" of Africa. For us it means government, business, education, industry, the professions, the arts, journalism. It means civil rights, international relations, automation, unemployment, retirement, leisure time, and moon shots. It means our total culture and all of its parts.

It is natural that this mission should rest largely with laymen. They must be the church's ambassadors in these newly recognized mission areas, because they are the ones who are familiar with the territory, conversant with the language, and at home with the cultural peculiarities of the particular segment of the society which must now be won for Christ. We must make certain that their intimate knowledge of the secular world is matched by their knowledge of and commitment to the Christian faith.

Full acceptance of this new concept of the church will involve a radical restructuring of it at the local level. If its purpose is to penetrate society with God's redeeming love, then it must organize itself to do exactly that. Familiar patterns of church and Sunday school, youth groups, and women's societies will have to be replaced with new ones better suited to the new demands.

Every change that is made should be the church's best response to this one question: "What is our mission and how can we best accomplish it?"

This involves a different set of concepts from those assumed by most of us. We must begin to think of our church as our denomination's *mission to* the city in which it is located rather than an *institution of* that city. It is sent *into* the city, but it is not *of* the city. It is *of* Christ. This means that the First Methodist Church of Landscape City should be in reality, if not in name, the Methodist mission *to* Landscape City.

Once that concept is grasped, another question becomes obvious. How many separate missions does a denomination have to one city? Surely our mission is not a babble of many voices. There must be a unified approach. Realization of this fact leads to a careful evaluation of the long-accepted policy of maintaining many churches in a single city. This multiple-church pattern of denominational life grew up under a now outdated concept of the church's mission. It was established when churches were expected to be within walking distance of their members. But if the church is to function as a mission to the whole city and the various cultural organisms within it, rather than as a group of separate institutions in the various geographical chunks of the city, it must accept some extreme changes in organization.

No one knows exactly what form these will take. If all the churches of a city begin to see themselves as a single mission, they will seek ways of getting maximum efficiency from their combined resources. They might begin by merging such organizations as their commissions on Christian social concerns. If the denomination is to give significant leadership to a city struggling with a race problem or divided on a school issue, it must move into the situation with its power harnessed and its purpose focused. This is possible if it has one commission, authorized as the church's "ambassadors" in this particular area. It is very unlikely if the denomination has a dozen different commissions from as many different churches, each approaching the problem from a different angle, some saying one thing and some another. Successful subunions of this type could be expected to lead to more groups following the same procedure until the denomination is geared to operate smoothly in one unified mission to the city.

As this approach develops, another fact begins to emerge: geographical areas are no longer the basic units of society. Cultural areas are. City dwellers seldom know their neighbors. Their lives revolve around social, business, political, or special interests involving people from many neighborhoods. These form the new locale of the church's mission. This is hard to visualize because "groups," "interests," and "functions" are hard to locate on a map. That's what makes the new mission of the church so challenging. It requires a maximum of creative imagination and ingenuity.

It also requires specialized leadership. Here again we must face a radical adjustment of traditional patterns. The ordained ministry must shift from a profession of "general practitioners" to a reservoir of "specialists." A denomination that previously placed ten separate ministers in ten separate churches at ten separate geographical locations in the city, all having had a general theological education and all seeking to give oversight to a total and complex church program, may still have ten ministers but with vastly different assignments. Each will be a specialist to give guidance as to the Christian strategy of approach in various aspects of the mission enterprise. A specialist in race problems will give guidance in that field. A labor specialist will train laymen to penetrate the blue-collar portion of the city's population, a group so frequently missed by our middle-class churches. Other ministers will specialize in the church's mission to politics or the arts or education. One will be the preacher, one the pastor, one the administrator. Particular specialists will be selected according to the need and more will be added as new needs develop and additional professional help seems necessary. These ministerial specialists will train, guide, and inspire the laymen who are the primary workers in fulfilling the mission of the church.

It must have been something like this that Paul envisioned when he wrote to the church at Ephesus, ". . . that some should be apostles, some prophets, some evangelists, some pastors and teachers, for the equipment of the saints, for the work of ministry, for building up the body of Christ . . ." (Eph. 4:11–12).

What might emerge from all of this is a denominational center in a city where the strategy for the Christian mission in that locality is carefully planned and from which lay ambassadors are dispatched. Here the total laity and clergy will come for the functions of the gathered church. To this place they will come to report on progress in their ambassadorial assignments. Here they will seek assistance in handling difficult problems, and here they will assemble for worship and study.

With the church reshaped somewhat along these lines, the religious life of the laymen would begin to fall into a weekly cycle that would look something like this:

Worship—Orders—Ministry—Report—Chores—Study—

Worship. Each seven days the cycle would be repeated. Such disciplined order in the layman's practice of religion has several marked advantages:

1. It is definite as opposed to the fuzziness that characterizes so much church activity.

2. It is simple and easy to understand and practice if one has the will to do so.

3. It is "chaste"—that is, free from distracting involvements, meaningless ceremony, or unnecessary activity.

4. It is focused. Everything in it points toward a goal. It leaves no room for meandering.

A quick look at the separate elements in such a week's Christian disciplines should be enough to give the feel of the new life it could bring to the layman.

Worship. As was stated in Chapter IV, the Sunday service is central for the Christian. Here the church gathers as one family for its most sacred function. One service is better than two. How sad that it should sometimes be necessary to divide the family for this weekly reunion.

Orders. This refers to the layman's ambassadorial assignment. Ordination is often referred to as ministerial "orders." Ministers and laymen alike need to recapture the sense of being under orders from Christ to do his work.

In a general way, the sermon, as discussed in Chapter V, should point up the job the churchman must do. This could be supplemented by the small-group approach in which laymen would ask one another, "How can each of us express the Christian truth contained in this week's sermon, as we proceed to our ambassadorial posts?" The various ministerial specialists would provide extensive help at this point. They would assume the responsibility for "the equipment of the saints" (Eph. 4:12), as Paul puts it. This might involve extensive training. In fact, training for the lay work of "mission" deserves a special designation of its own. However, I have not included it along with the other focus points of the layman's week because it is subject to many variations. Some of it might be done in concentrated summer sessions for the training of laymen in the strategy of mission. Some of it might be handled through personal consultation with the ministerial specialists. And some of it would be done naturally and routinely in connection with "orders" or "study."

Mission. When the layman has crystallized in his own mind what his orders are for the week, he will proceed to carry them out. This is his mission, a part of the church's ministry to the city and to the world. Most of the week will be spent at this task which is away from the church building and from the company of church friends.

Report. Anyone out on an assignment needs to report on his progress from time to time. The knowledge that he is to do this increases his sense of responsibility and reminds him of the importance of what he is doing. It also gives him the assurance there is something to tie to, someone from whom to seek guidance and help.

Some of this reporting would be done directly to the ministerial "specialists" who are administering the work of mission. Most of it, however, would occur in small groups, composed of people involved in similar assignments. Great power can be generated in a group whose members share their experiences and seek counsel from one another. This is a deep human need that has been largely overlooked by the church since the old testimony meetings went out of fashion. Groups of this kind are more vital than study groups because they bring knowledge to life by putting it into action. They are more significant than fellowship groups because they enrich their relationship by adding purpose to their togetherness. They are more constructive than therapy groups because, to the freedom to share their feelings, they add the assurance that they are involved in a great mission.

Chores. There is work to be done in the church organization itself as well as "out there" in the world. As was indicated in Chapter IX, each layman should have some part in doing the work that is necessary to keep the organization going, and care for the needs of fellow Christians who are sick or discouraged.

Care. No work within the organization is more important than loving care of the members themselves. I have already pointed out that anyone joining the church for the sake of the personal services it is said to give its members has hitched his wagon to the wrong star. However, a minimum human requirement of any fellowship is concern for its own members. Even a service club sends flowers to its members who are sick, and the public school checks up on its absentees. The church should do no less.

Pastoral care is a privilege in which every layman should share. Here again ministerial specialists will give guidance and training, but the renewed church will be characterized by concern for all the members for one another. With the regularity of the Boy Scout's legendary "good deed" daily, every churchman should devote some time each week to what Paul calls "building up the body of Christ, until we all attain to the unity of the faith and of the knowledge of the Son of God, to mature manhood, to the measure of the stature of the fullness of Christ . . ." (Eph. 4:12–13).

Study. An alert layman is always eager to learn. We emphasized the importance of study in Chapters III and VI. The church should have a strong program of education, geared toward the accomplishment of the church's central mission. This duty of the layman might be combined with "Orders" or "Report" in accordance with the particular church's need.

Organized on such a cycle, the church should experience new life and the layman find new joy in his faith. Each element in it is there for the good reason that it is of major importance. Other things traditionally associated with the church are missing for the equally good reason that they are of secondary importance. The elements of churchmanship that have been highlighted here might be thought of as the beat in the rhythm of Christian living. The total pattern has been suggested as a possible way for a church in revolution to move forward constructively. It is to answer the critics by saying: "Your criticisms are basic. But your despair is groundless. Church renewal is long overdue;

we are recovering our purpose by returning to scripture, and we are restoring our relevance by reshaping the institution to fit the demands of a reshaped culture." Besides being an answer to the critics, this suggested new pattern is also a warning to those most responsible for their criticism. It says to them that clutching the past is as hopeless as embracing the dead, and we will participate in such an activity no longer. But neither will we abandon the church to the care of the grave diggers. Radical change is coming but we are not waiting for it. We are directing it.

Let no one underestimate the dangers involved in taking such a stand. No one launching a bold new venture has any guarantee of its success. If he has, it is neither bold nor new. It is not even a venture. What we are talking about requires courage. There is the ugly risk of failure in it. We expect to worship the Christian God, live the Christian life, and walk in the Christian way, to be sure. But that isn't as safe as it sounds. Rather, it is precisely where the risk comes.

It is a truism to say that the Christian God is the true God; the Christian life is the good life; the Christian way is the right way. Yet these assertions, while undeniable from the Christian standpoint, are deceptively reassuring. It is too easy to assume that the "true God" favors us, that the "good life" is the easy life, and that the "right way" is the way we happen to be going. This is the lazy logic that many laymen lie down in. It gives rise to the heresy that peace of mind is automatic for those who love the Lord and that positive thinking opens the doors of opportunity as effortlessly as an electronic eye throws back the doors of the best hotels and supermarkets.

This common fallacy characterizes a large number, perhaps even a majority, of today's laymen. No matter how much objective evidence or personal experience accumulates on the other side of the question, they persist in the belief that God is busy doing favors for them. Presumably this is because they deserve it. Thus they accept the great doctrines of the Christian faith and twist them into weird distortions. In their hands, the love of God becomes the power that favors them with wealth when others are poor. The forgiveness of God becomes the assurance that sin doesn't matter unless it is the other fellow who is committing it. The cross becomes the convenient doctrine that we won't have to suffer for our sins since Jesus paid it all. And salvation becomes nothing more than the process by which people come over on our side.

This brings us near the center of the infection the experts are talking about when they say that the church is sick, and it explains the hopelessness many of them feel when they think of the prospects of shaping up this undisciplined, self-righteous, uninformed, and misdirected group of people into an army of the Lord. It is understandable that so many of them conclude that it would be easier to start over with a new batch. How do you go about convincing people who expect Christianity to heal them that it is more likely to hurt them? How do you get people who are accustomed to turning to Christ for comfort to carry an uncomfortable cross? How do you persuade people who have twisted their faith to fit their deformities to stop tampering with the Christian gospel and start living by it?

The layman who would live a meaningful life within the institution of the church must come to terms with these questions. He must orient himself to the reality of the cross. He must learn, not academically only, but in harsh experience that to stand up for God is to get knocked down by man, that to live by strict rules of Christian ethics among people who have read a different rule book is to offer oneself as the sacrificial lamb, and that to walk in the way that leads to Life is to walk alone, or in the company of the unacceptable.

Admittedly one who stands up for God is not invariably knocked down by man; godliness is sometimes honored. Jesus was loved and listened to, even worshiped. But he was also crucified. So while Christian living brings its rewards and satisfactions, it is hazardous. If today's churchmen are not encountering the hazards, then today's churchmen are not living the Christian life. Nothing the New Testament teaches is clearer than that to embrace Christianity is to face hostility. A follower of Christ must expect persecution.

But today's churchmen don't. They expect honor from their children, respect from their neighbors, acceptance by their community, and a discount on everything they purchase in the name of the church. They do not expect hostility.

This reversal of the proper expectations of the Christian leads to a misreading of the signs. When churchmen receive the honor, respect, acceptance, and economic advantages they expect, they conclude that their righteousness is confirmed. Good behavior, they feel, is rewarded with favors. If the favors come, that proves the good behavior.

Similarly criticism, attack, and accusation are clear evidence to them that the churchmen involved are radicals who have infiltrated the cozy community of the church. They are thought of as troublemakers who ought to be frozen out of the organization.

Of course being in trouble is not proof of Christian behavior any more than is staying out of it. Nevertheless, any Christian layman who has not been "persecuted for righteousness' sake" (Matt. 5:10) had better start his Christian life over again. Instead of asking himself if he is good and concluding that he is (or that if he is not, it is only because he is human), he should ask himself if he has been persecuted, and if not, why not?

We recognize the dangers of a persecution complex, and we know that the person who wants to be abused so that he can feel noble, is sick. We are also quick to see the folly of rash action that stimulates unnecessary retaliation. But we have been slow to admit that we are more afraid of persecution than of a persecution complex and have hidden our cowardliness under the guise of considered judgment.

If he is to be effective, the Christian layman must

take a fresh look at the dark side of his faith. The cross is at the center of Christianity and the cross is a symbol of failure. It reminds us that Jesus tried to win the people with his love and was crushed by their hatred. We know, of course, that in a wider sense he merely lost a battle and won the war. He triumphed over the cross. This is a part of what we are talking about when, as in one of our affirmations of faith we declare our belief in "the final triumph of righteousness." But the triumph is not yet won. The cross is still in the world—stark, rough, ugly, and destructive. It comes first. The triumph later. That's why we say that the Christian layman must know the possibility of failure and risk it.

That means that he will support the work of the church in Communist-dominated lands in spite of the risk that the buildings he helps to finance may subsequently be taken over and used by the Communists. He will help to provide scholarships not only for students who "show great promise of success" but also for those who stand a good chance of failing. He will defend the person whom his friends attack. He will point out the rightness of unpopular causes. He will seek rather than shun the company of those who have a reputation for being troublemakers, immoral, crude, or criminal. He will attack evil among his closest friends as readily as he attacks the evil of some alien government or criminal element. He will put principle ahead of politeness and practice personal piety in social settings where it is considered discourteous. He will be honest even if it costs him a promotion. He will be selfless in the goodwill he extends to others even when they take advantage of it. He will speak his political convictions although every bumper sticker in the parking lot tries to shout him down. He will be open and persistent in his efforts to make advertising honest, to base business on sound principles of Christian ethics, to develop a culture that nourishes the best in all men, and to create government that embodies the Christian principle of peace on earth, goodwill to men.

Doing this, the layman will not emerge unscathed. Sometimes his heroism will be honored. Sometimes the rightness of his cause will be recognized and popular support will swing his way. Sometimes he will have the satisfaction of having won a few to a deeper Christian life. But among these successes will be some failures. Often the point of view he expresses will be misunderstood or misinterpreted. Often he will be painted with the same unsavory reputation with which those he seeks to help have been colored. Often the cause he defends will be defeated. But in a sense all of this is beside the point. He must be faithful to the gospel. God will tally the score.

In all of this he will be following a spirit more than a rule book.

You can't get your hands on a spirit. It is real nonetheless, and of major importance to any layman who would live effectively within the institution of the church. Awareness of this is what does most to save the church from mere institutionalism.

Among the songs of social protest that have become a part of American folk music in recent years is Bob Dylan's "Blowin' in the Wind." Commenting on the song, which raises a series of questions about how long it will be before basic human rights are granted to all men and human brotherhood becomes a reality, Dylan says that "the first way to answer these questions . . . is by asking them." He gives no solutions for the problems but suggests that the answer is coming; it is "blowin' in the wind." He hints that there is an invisible force of righteousness moving in the world. The Christian faith says about the same thing. Dylan calls it the wind. The Bible calls it the Holy Spirit.

Moses sensed its presence and led the children of Israel from tyranny to freedom by following the guidance of that one "who is invisible" (Heb. 11:27). The Psalmist was aware of such a presence and praised the Lord who "ridest on the wings of the wind" (Ps. 104:3). Jesus described the Spirit of God as a wind "that blows where it wills" (John

3:8). And the disciples at Pentecost were caught in the path of it when the Holy Spirit descended upon them "like the rush of a mighty wind" (Acts 2:2). The Book of Acts is the dramatic account of what happened to these men when they were led by a power they did not see with their eyes and answered commands they did not hear with their ears. Their world, like ours, was dark and full of problems, but for them as for the folk singer, "the answer [was] blowin' in the wind."

Many people have experienced this power. John Henry Newman knew it as the "kindly light" that leads "amid th'encircling gloom," and confessed that while sometimes in his selfishness he turned away from it, when he turned back it was still the power that led him on. Benjamin Franklin declared his conviction that "God governs in the affairs of men" and that nations succeed or fail in response to the movement of His unseen hand. Arnold Toynbee sees the mysterious rise and fall of civilizations through history as the turning of the wheels that carry forward some "divine plan" that is consistently "making headway." Victor Hugo affirmed that Napoleon's defeat at Waterloo was not due to superior military force arrayed against him, but to the fact that he got in the way of the Spirit of God and was blown down. "Napoleon had been denounced by the Infinite," he affirmed, "and his fall had been decided on. He embarrassed God." In like manner, former Prime Minister Macmillan explained the collapse of one after another of Africa's powerful colonial empires in a short fifteen-year period by saying simply, "The wind of change began to blow." And Martin Luther King who, without guns or bombs, high office or personal wealth, is shaking this nation down to basic principles, is doing it by telling the people they must rely on the unseen power of moral force and the invisible hand of God will sustain them. He compares the movement with which he is identified with the coming in of the tide which no man can stop.

Morally and spiritually, today's world, like the world of

the Genesis story, is "without form and void" (Gen. 1:2), and there is "darkness . . . upon the face of the deep" (Gen. 1:2). We are haunted with a thousand questions: What kind of world will our children inherit? Where will our affluence lead us? Will hatred ever give way to love? How soon will our narrow nationalism be exposed for what it is and our selfish striving look ugly even to us? The folk singer says that "the answer is blowin' in the wind." Perhaps he is right. "The Spirit of God was moving over the face of the waters . . . and there was light" (Gen. 1:2–3).

There is nothing with which the Christian layman is concerned that is of greater significance than this indefinite, unpredictable thing called the Spirit, which comes "like a thief in the night" (I Thess. 5:2).

It catches people by surprise. Segregationists for example. They didn't feel the wind blowing in their faces until it reached hurricane proportions. And some of them still think they can tame the storm and confine it to the black man's corner. Perhaps not until its fury has left them desolate will they stand by some monument honoring a martyred civil-rights worker, or by a "new Jerusalem" rising out of Watts's "charcoal alley" and there, like the bewildered centurion on the hill where Jesus was crucified, admit at last that they were defeated before they began because God was in this storm. And in their defeat they will know what the Psalmist meant when he said, "The wicked . . . are like chaff which the wind drives away" (Ps. 1:4). You can't fight the Spirit of God and win.

Not even the Communists can do it. They can preempt church property, assassinate ministers, and brainwash Christian laymen, but they can't keep the Spirit of God from moving in the hearts of the people. After the Communists had taken over China, a Christian doctor, preparing to operate on a party official turned aside, as was his practice preceding every surgery, to pray for a moment. As he did so, he heard the Communist official say, "Doctor, pray for me." American scientists involved in recent international scientific gatherings report that their Russian counterparts, in private conversation with them, have been asking what they believe about God and immortality, and how they find spiritual resources for daily living. It would appear that the Spirit of God has been doing a little brainwashing of Its own.

The Christian layman learns to depend on this Spirit. He is like the surfer who, after dragging his board through resistant waters, connects with the wave he can ride to shore like a conquering hero, with all the power of the ocean harnessed to carry him to his destination. The mysterious muscle of the seas is his to use because his destination is the same as the destination of the wave. That's what it means to discover the winds of God and move with them.

Let no one be deceived. There is danger in that ride. The surfer is running risks. He may get hurt, and he knows it. He also knows that the danger gives the ride its exultation!

To be caught within God's Spirit and be swept along toward His high goals is not a sport for weaklings. Anyone who wants the challenge should also know the risks. There is the danger of misunderstanding, loss of status, sacrifice of job. There is the chance one's family, too, will suffer and one's reputation meet with smears beyond repair. There is the risk of sickness caused by overwork, or accident since there's so little time for hazards to be charted. And then of course, the chance of being victimized by the direct attack of some misguided soul who thinks his calling is to trip the sons of God, defeat their cause, and nail them to some cross.

Of course the risks are great. That's what the cross is all about. But somehow, when the wind has filled our sail, the dangers that we feared become the challenges that call us on. Our Christ was crucified and his disciples stoned and thrown in jail, or burned at stakes to warn the weak and serve as beacon lights to challenge men of strength.

Through the years it's always been the same. They

laughed at Francis, cast young Luther from the church, descended on John Wesley in great mobs. A Midwest doctor, buying land that none but whites had ever held, was told he wasn't wanted, since his skin was black. But his church stood by him, and in the standing took the blows along with him. A minister in Mississippi left his post and ran the risk of being unemployed when the Spirit said: "The church is for all men and no man can be excluded." Farther south along the Gulf, a father walked through howling mobs of ranting racists with his small girl's hand in his because some Force invisible had said he must. And in the West where segregation is more real than apparent, some churchmen, responding to the Spirit's call, have moved from suburban comfort to the ghetto to be identified with those less fortunate than they.

Each of these has learned this mighty truth, that it is better to face opposition and be right although he stands alone, than to melt into a crowd that has lost its way. And one who has caught the answer in the wind has found a joy that transcends life and death. He knows it is for this that we were born: to listen for the Wind and travel with It.

In times like these men seek in vain for something firm to stand on, a bit of earth they know to be secure. But the Christian knows security is in the Wind. It moves. "For all who are led by the Spirit of God are sons of God" (Rom. 8:14).